£ 1.90

EARNEST ENQUIRERS AFTER TRUTH

EARNEST ENQUIRERS AFTER TRUTH

A Gifford Anthology

EXCERPTS FROM GIFFORD LECTURES 1888-1968

SELECTED BY

BERNARD E. JONES

London

GEORGE ALLEN & UNWIN LTD

RUSKIN HOUSE   MUSEUM STREET

© *George Allen & Unwin Ltd,* 1970
ISBN 0 04 108001 7

PRINTED IN GREAT BRITAIN
in 10 *point Plantin type*
BY T. & A. CONSTABLE LTD
EDINBURGH

The Bequest

I having been for many years deeply and firmly convinced that
the true knowledge of God, that is, of the All, of the First and
Only Cause, that is the One and Only Substance and Being, and
the true and felt knowledge (not mere nominal knowledge) of
the relations of man and of the universe to Him, and of the
true foundations of all ethics and morals, being, I say, convinced
that this knowledge, when really felt and acted on, is the means
of man's highest well-being, and the security of his upward
progress, I have resolved from the 'residue' of my estate
as aforesaid, to institute and found, in connection, if possible
with the Scottish Universities, lectureships or classes for
the promotion of the study of the said subjects, and for the
teaching and diffusing of sound views regarding them, among
the whole population of Scotland. . . .

The lecturers appointed shall be subjected to no test of any
kind . . . they may be of any religion or way of thinking, or, as
is sometimes said, they may be of no religion, or they may be
so-called sceptics or agnostics or freethinkers, provided only
that the 'patrons' will use diligence to secure that they be able
reverent men, true thinkers, sincere lovers of and earnest
inquirers after truth.

ADAM GIFFORD

The full text of the will, from which this and other excerpts
are taken, is printed in the Edinburgh University *Calendar*,
1888-89.

CONTENTS

Introduction

When a volume is described as Gifford Lectures the experienced reader will expect to find a fairly lengthy and erudite work that will not be particularly comprehensible to the man in the street. Indeed sometimes even the student fights shy and looks for some useful 'digest'. Yet the one who founded the lectureships hoped that the lectures would be appreciated by 'the whole community without matriculation' and that they would be both 'public and popular'. He envisaged the possibility that the lectures or parts of them might be produced at a cheap selling price so that the whole population might benefit. This anthology is an attempt to show the variety of ways in which the 'Earnest Enquirers after Truth', appointed from time to time by the Gifford Trustees, have fulfilled their task. Excerpts have been chosen which, it is hoped, will be comprehensible to the ordinary man who wants to know what the Gifford Lectures are all about, and which may prove a useful introduction to the student.

As a result of the stroke of a pen in the year 1885 about 110 experts have been set talking for approximately twenty hours each and over 130 volumes of lectures have been published. In 1888 the first Gifford lectures were delivered and for eighty years and more Gifford lecturers have been appointed in the four older Scottish universities to talk in general about 'God, the Infinite, the All, the First and Only Cause'. The last will and testament of Adam Gifford, signed by him on the twenty-first day of August 1885, and witnessed by a medical doctor and a cab driver, must be one of the strangest and most fascinating wills ever executed. Adam Gifford was born in Edinburgh on February 29, 1820, and died on January 20, 1887.

In a little-known memoir[1] his brother tells us that Adam Gifford was a bright boy who mastered his lessons easily and because of his persistent curiosity and acute intelligence he was given the nickname 'The Philosopher'. Some of his equally precocious friends established a society for asking and answering questions but young Adam Gifford declined to join. Evidently he preferred to think out the problems for himself, or, maybe, setting questions had a greater appeal for him. At all events decades later he set the questions which generations of

[1] John Gifford, *Recollections of a Brother, Adam Gifford, one of the Senators of the College of Justice in Scotland under the title Lord Gifford*. Printed for the family, 1891.

scholars—philosophers, scientists and theologians—were to attempt to answer in the course of their Gifford lectures.

As a young man he was a Sunday school teacher and assisted at the ragged school at the Cowgate, Edinburgh but he sat loosely to the credal formulations of organised religion. He entered the legal profession and was finally appointed judge at the age of forty-nine. He would thus find little difficulty in drawing up his own will, and seems to have enjoyed the legal exercise. He brought to his thinking about religion the same keen mind that he exercised in the law court, and he wanted other people to think clearly about religion too. Religion was more than an intellectual adventure for Adam Gifford. He was concerned that the knowledge of God should be 'true and felt' knowledge—not mere nominal knowledge. He was anxious that this knowledge should be available to ordinary folk beyond the world of dons and students and that they should be able to attend and understand the lectures.

'The lectures shall be public and popular, that is, open not only to students of the Universities, but to the whole community without matriculation, as I think that the subject should be studied and known by all, whether receiving University instruction or not.'

Lord Gifford lectured from time to time on a wide variety of subjects and in a little book of lectures,[1] again published for private circulation, is one addressed to the Edinburgh Y.M.C.A. in 1878. The High Court judge gave this advice to young men, and this affords some idea of what Adam Gifford expected of the ordinary young men of his day.

'Now I take this opportunity of saying to you—young men, keenly desirous of mental and moral elevation, don't neglect Metaphysics! The Sciences of the Mind and the doctrine of the Unseen and the Universal! . . I make no apology for asking you to *think*. Your presence here declares your readiness and anxiety to do so. No truth of the smallest value can be attained without thought, without thought often painfully earnest and protracted.'

These young men were warned not to take too much notice of the votaries and champions of the physical sciences, who arrogantly claim for them alone the name of sciences—

'. . . as if the polar collocations and whirling vortices of enchanted atoms were all that ultimately men could really know!'

Adam Gifford believed that it was possible to build up a *Science* of God without any reference to special revelation. His great hero,

---

[1] Adam Gifford, *Lectures Delivered on Various Occasions*, Frankfurt, 1889.

Spinoza, had set out his beliefs about God in mathematical form, beginning with definitions and axioms and moving on to propositions and corollaries with the periodical Q.E.D. to conclude each section. This appealed to Adam Gifford, who was a man of his own century, a century of new scientific discoveries, a century to be remembered for the controversy between upholders of scientific theories and defenders of the Bible. It seemed to Adam Gifford that a new evangelism was needed. If men and women were to be convinced of religious truth it would be by means of scientific demonstration rather than any appeal to infallible revelation.

'I wish the lecturers to treat their subject as a strictly natural science, the greatest of all possible sciences, indeed, in one sense, the only science, that of Infinite Being, without reference to or reliance upon any supposed special exceptional or so-called miraculous revelation. I wish it studied just as astronomy or chemistry is.'

The will has been criticized on the grounds that it anticipates the conclusions the lecturers shall draw. This is partly true, but while it may be said that Lord Gifford was himself so sure of the existence of God that he could not conceive of any other verdict, he wanted all the evidence presented. He wrote:

'The lecturers appointed shall be subject to no test of any kind, and shall not be required to take an oath, or to emit or subscribe any declaration of belief, or to make any promise of any kind; they may be of any denomination whatever, or of no denomination at all . . . they may be of any religion or way of thinking, or . . . they may be of no religion . . . provided only that the "patrons" will use diligence to secure that they be able reverent men, true thinkers, sincere lovers of and earnest inquirers after truth.'

Further he declared:

'The lecturers shall be under no restraint whatever in their theme; for example, they may freely discuss (and it may be well to do so) . . . whether God is under any or what limitations, and so on, as I am persuaded that nothing but good can result from free discussion.'

Many of the lecturers have demurred at the conditions imposed, Karl Barth most of all. It was not that he did not believe in the existence of God but that he did not believe in the possibility of natural theology. But he need not have been troubled, for Lord Gifford wanted all the evidence presented. The Gifford lecturer must be as free as the witness in the law-court. The High Court judge wanted the truth about God, the whole truth and nothing but the truth.

Adam Gifford was paralysed for some years before his death and later was confined to the house. He would retire to his room with books as his companions, especially the works of Spinoza. Yet we must not think of him as a man whose interests in religion were purely academic. He was deeply religious and some of his thoughts during this period are recorded in the memoir written by his brother.

'I think I have seen more clearly many things about God since I have been laid aside. In the night I often can't sleep and I follow out new trains of thought about Him.'

'To be happier or wiser, that just means to have more of God.'

'He is infinite, how can our finite minds grasp His Being? But it is not wrong to go on in our thinking as far as we can.'

It was during this period that he drew up his will. A man of his own day, he lived in a world of scientific promise and philosophical idealism. He was utterly certain that religion is not merely a human experience induced by man's desires; nevertheless he wanted the whole matter investigated so that faith might be distinguished from credulity and religion from superstition—and this for all classes of society, not just for the intellectual elite.

'My desire and hope is that these lectureships and lectures may promote and advance among all classes of the community the true knowledge of Him . . . Whom truly to know is life everlasting.'

These sound views concerning the subjects described were not only to be diffused 'among all classes of the community' but among 'the whole population of Scotland'. To this end the patrons

'. . . if and when they see fit may make grants from the free income of the endowments for or towards the publication in a cheap form of any of the lectures, or any part thereof, or abstracts thereof, which they may think likely to be useful.'

Thus Adam Gifford set out to benefit the whole population of Scotland but the whole world of philosophical theology is his debtor. One can hardly conceive that there is a university in any land which does not have on the shelves of its library at least some volumes of Gifford lectures. Year by year the discussion goes on in the four Scottish universities in the strange continuing Gifford society for asking questions about God and answering them within the limitations imposed by the subject itself.

At the completion of the first eighty years of Gifford lectures it is appropriate to ask how the venture is going and to what extent Adam

Gifford's wishes have been fulfilled. The wording of the will has often been criticized but it is a tribute to its author that year after year lecturers can still find some new facet of the subject or some new approach to an old theme. The company that has passed through the Gifford witness-box has indeed been distinguished. The great names of science, philosophy and theology are in the lists, J. S. Haldane, Eddington, Heisenberg and Weizsacker; William James, Bergson, Alexander and Whitehead; Barth and Brunner, Temple and Tillich. There was Andrew Lang, a maker of fairy tales, Albert Schweitzer, musician-missionary and philosopher-theologian, two archbishops, three bishops, able reverent men—no women as yet—true thinkers, earnest inquirers after truth!

Adam Gifford was not the first to describe natural theology as a science. In the sixteenth century Raymond de Sebonde had described natural theology as 'a science that is accessible alike to laymen and clerks . . . and can be had in less than a month and without trouble'. Natural theology has been seen as the adventures of man in search of God, while the opponents of natural theology have seen their gospel only in terms of the Advent of God in search of man. Adam Gifford stressed the former without denying the possibility of the latter. None of the Gifford lecturers have taken the somewhat naïve view of natural theology held by Raymond de Sebonde and later by Paley. Even those who were themselves confessed believers have recognized that there is no easy way with unbelievers. It is doubtful if even Lord Gifford thought that his lecturers could ever do more than show that belief in God is a not unreasonable conclusion. C. P. Tiele, an early Gifford lecturer said that the purpose of natural theology was to subject religion to 'unprejudiced investigation'. Another early lecturer described the task as 'construing' religion rather than constructing it. A more recent lecturer spoke of its function as 'thinking dispassionately about religion'. C. A. Campbell writes:

'Natural theology seeks a rational answer to the question "Is religion true?" And if so, in what precise sense?'

The contemporary discussion is dominated by the problem of language and of the possibility of God-talk, but it was a Gifford lecturer, R. B. Haldane, who set the two fundamental questions in the first years of the century,

'The first is: What do we mean by *God*? The second is: How, in the light that in the twentieth century philosophy has cast on Reality, must we conceive and speak of Him?'

The publication of *Honest to God* in 1963 led to a far wider interest in natural theology but many of the problems raised in recent discussions have found their place in the Gifford lectures of earlier years. The problem of the *'up-there-ness'* of God, which played an important part in the *Honest to God* discussion, was dealt with by Edwyn Bevan in the early thirties. In a period dominated by problems of religious language we may recall the dictum of Max Muller, the first Glasgow lecturer:

'A study of language is absolutely necessary as an introduction to the study of philosophy as well as of religion.'

In the thirties and forties natural theology fell into disrepute attacked by positivists, logical and theological. Natural theology was described as the sick man of Europe and the opinion expressed that it might be as well to let him die quietly.[1] But man, the God-haunted animal as he has been called, goes on asking questions about God. There is a place for natural theology even if its task is only that of framing the questions. This is how Tillich saw it, but Adam Gifford asked for natural theology in the widest sense of that term, and the second section of our anthology reveals something of the breadth of interpretation.

It is understandable that in the early years there should have been some confusion between natural theology and natural religion. Because the appeal to any so-called miraculous revelation was forbidden, the trustees turned to scholars such as E. B. Tylor, Max Muller and Andrew Lang, whose knowledge of primitive and eastern religions enabled them to give an account of some of 'man's conceptions of God, their origin, nature and truth'. C. P. Tiele's attempt to establish a *Science of Religion* led naturally on to what has become known as comparative religion. Sir James Frazer, R. R. Marett, and more recently Alexander MacBeath studied the religions of simple folk. Others turned to Greek and Roman religion. All these studies were within the scope of Lord Gifford's intention but too often lecturers were content to give an account of the origin and nature of man's conceptions of God, while avoiding the thorny problem of their truth. Similarly some lecturers took the opportunity of presenting historical studies, tracing the growth of man's conceptions of God through the development of Christian thought. It is possible to trace the history of natural theology from the earliest Babylonian and Greek beginnings through the medieval period to the moderns without reference to other works than Gifford lectures, Etienne Gilson having filled with his *Spirit of Medieval Philosophy* a strange hiatus left by the protestant historians.

Gradually the inhibitions felt about dealing with the Christian faith

---

[1] See *Soundings*, ed. A. R. Vidler (1962), p. 3.

were overcome. It is true that no lecturer must *rely* on any supposed special exceptional or so-called miraculous revelation, but in the spirit of William Temple's *Nature, Man and God* he may bring the Christian faith to the bar of reason. Ideas of what is natural and supernatural, general and special revelation, have changed since Lord Gifford's day The Gifford series would have been the poorer without the contribution of the Christian theologians. Nevertheless the wording of Lord Gifford's will has precluded any straightforward dogmatic presentation of the case. The nature of faith has frequently been discussed and a section of the anthology gathers together some of the interpretations of what Adam Gifford called true and felt knowledge of God. Diverse views of the relationship of revelation to religion find their place in another section.

Some thinkers have spurned the Gifford Lectures as being disguised apologetic rather than true philosophy. It would be difficult to think that philosophers like Bergson and A. E. Taylor, Alexander and Whitehead, would have reached other conclusions or expressed themselves differently had they been lecturing under another foundation. What is clear is that Lord Gifford hoped that the lectures would indeed promote and advance the true knowledge of God but this is different from distorting the evidence in the hope of persuading the jury to reach a particular verdict. It is right to subject religious faith to the most stringent investigation, but, to continue the analogy of the Gifford law-court, there must be a summing up and a verdict, even if it is the Scots verdict of not proven. This incidentally was the specific wording used by John Laird[1] though he added that if plausibility were enough the theistic view was more plausible than other metaphysical views. In this sense natural theology can be the ally of faith. H. H. Farmer saw natural theology as 'the attempt to present theism as a reasonable and satisfying (indeed, the most reasonable and satisfying), though not logically demonstrable world-view.' Admittedly there are dangers in any kind of apologetic but earnest inquirers after truth will be aware of the snares of wishful thinking.

Lord Gifford's desire that natural theology should be studied as a natural science just as astronomy or chemistry has provided considerable difficulty. The scientists who have been called as witnesses have in general acknowledged that the questions posed go beyond their responsibilities as scientists. It was inevitable that scientists should be appointed—the high priests of the twentieth-century temple of knowledge whose foundations were laid in the nineteenth—but all of them: Driesch, J. S. Haldane, Eddington, Sherrington, Heisenberg, Weizsacker and the rest have reported that 'the Infinite, the All, the First

[1] See Selection 18

and Only Cause' dwells not in temples erected by the scientists. The first lecturer at Edinburgh had no doubts on this score when he wrote in reference to newly devised American telescopes:

'The very tallest American with the very tallest of telescopes will never be able to say that he spied out God.'

The scientist's evidence must be called but the enquiry goes beyond the how to the why. Some have shown that scientific knowledge is not incompatible with religious belief and some have gone so far as to show how they themselves have been able to reach beyond scientific knowledge to a theistic metaphysic or a personal faith. Eddington spoke of the jigsaw puzzle being constructed by the scientist which might present a different picture from day to day. Only at a risk, he said, can this picture be used for purposes beyond science. Heisenberg spoke of a developing scepticism among scientists concerning scepticism itself. Michael Polanyi pointed the way to a deeper perception of knowledge beyond the reaches of scientific language. It is not easy to treat natural theology just as astronomy or chemistry. Astronomy and chemistry begin by assuming the existence of the subject matter of the enquiry; natural theology must question the very existence of God. It is probably a misunderstanding of Adam Gifford's intention to suggest that he thought that scientific study could yield certain knowledge of God. He wanted the same careful analytic method to be applied to thinking about religion as in any science.

The most exciting of the early attempts to understand the nature of religion was undoubtedly William James's *Varieties of Religious Experience*, which has become a classic. He used the then infant science of psychology to study religious phenomena and established the truth, sometimes forgotten, that the ground of religion is indeed religious experience rather than rational argument. The wheel has gone full circle and in one of the most recently published series of lectures Sir Alister Hardy appeals for a natural theology that is 'a science of man's religious behaviour', by which he means a serious study of all that goes by the name of religious experience. Any study of 'the Infinite, the All, the First and only Cause' must of course involve a study of all that goes by the name of science, but what William James provided and what Sir Alister Hardy asks for is probably nearer to what Lord Gifford envisaged when he spoke of the parallel of astronomy and chemistry.

Adam Gifford recognized that belief in God involved obligations and duties and he included as possible subject matter of the lectures, 'The Nature and Foundation of Ethics or Morals'. This has led to a variety of approaches illustrated in the tenth section of the anthology. There have been some straightforward ethical studies such as Ross's

Foundations of Ethics or Austin Farrer's *Freedom of the Will*. Bishop Gore dealt with comparative ethics and Bishop Hensley Henson lectured on *Christian Morality, Natural, Developing, Final*. Three attempts have been made to link moral and religious experience; W. R. Sorley lectured on *Moral Values and the Idea of God* during the first world war; A. E. Taylor expounded *The Faith of a Moralist* in the twenties; De Burgh wrote *From Morality to Religion* in the thirties. These three works, each in its own way, presents a strong case for a moral argument for the existence of God.

The destiny of man has provided another fruitful line of enquiry. In its time, in an idealist context, Bosanquet's work on *The Value and Destiny of the Individual* was most influential. From an American standpoint Josiah Royce offered a similar service in *The World and the Individual*, while Niebuhr's *Nature and Destiny of Man* served a later generation with a different philosophical outlook. Modern thought has turned its attention to an examination of the personal and John Macmurray's two volumes on personality and personal relationships are outstanding. The ultimate destiny of man in an afterlife has provided occasional subject for discussion. Pringle-Pattison devoted a series of lectures to *The Idea of Immortality* and Sir James Frazer studied beliefs in immortality among primitive peoples.

Year after year in the four universities the earnest inquirers after truth have continued their work. Religion has been discussed by the anthropologist, the psychologist, the sociologist and the historian. The scientists have examined the world order to find what evidence there is of deity. The moral philosophers have investigated man's moral experience with a view to finding whether God is indeed a necessary postulate. Philosophers have examined metaphysical systems and constructed more in the attempt to solve the problem of theism. Other philosophers have examined and re-examined the traditional arguments for the existence of God, while the theologians, with few exceptions, have been prepared to put faith to the test of rational enquiry.

With the exception of a few who have avoided the ultimate issue the lecturers have attempted, in one way or another, to answer the two questions:

What kind of knowledge of God can unaided reason reach?
and
How far can unaided reason verify the assertions of faith?

The answers have been varied, Barth disallowing any possibility of help from reason, others like Brunner and Tillich allowing a vital if limited contribution, others again assigning a greater importance to the impartial investigation made by reason. There is sufficient unanimity

19

for us to assert that there is still need for such a study as natural theology, only a shadow of that study envisaged by Raymond de Sebonde and less influential perhaps than Lord Gifford thought it to be, but yet an indispensable discipline.

It is no longer justifiable to speak of natural theology as the sick man of Europe. This is not the verdict of the Gifford specialists. There is not only reasonable expectation of life but promise of a ripe old age. The patient must not attempt as much as he did in his younger days, but he is still fit for the less ambitious but nevertheless arduous task of bringing reason to bear on religious faith. The changing climate of the theological world is also auspicious for him. There is today a readiness to re-examine long established theological positions. Church leaders themselves have given publicity to the doubts and difficulties of the ordinary man. In a theological situation where it is almost a virtue to doubt, natural theology can only flourish. While there are those who want to *think* about their religion and not just to accept it blindly there will be a place for the natural theologian, the man who is prepared to examine by the impartial light of reason the claims of religion whether they be based on so-called miraculous revelation or human speculation. And because of the generosity and foresight of Adam Gifford the four Scottish universities can continue to appoint 'able, reverent men, true thinkers, sincere lovers of and earnest inquirers after truth' to fulfil this task.

The extracts have been gathered together around a number of themes suggested by phrases or paragraphs from the last will and testament of Lord Gifford. For the most part selections have been made as being typical of the particular lecturer's contribution, though in a few cases extracts have been included for the secondary reason that they contain quotations from some of the great thinkers of the past. Plato, Aristotle, Aquinas, Hume, Kant and Hegel, to mention but a few, have spoken many times through Gifford lecturers. Some footnotes in the original texts have been omitted but only where the interpretation is unaffected. Professional philosophers may well have reservations concerning anthologies such as this for selection involves the risk that a man's philosophy may be judged by a paragraph or two. Yet great thoughts can be expressed in a paragraph and this anthology may enable some who have never opened a volume of Gifford lectures to share thoughts that first found expression through the Gifford bequest, introducing them to the weightier volumes from which the extracts have been taken. In this way Lord Gifford's expressed desire may find some fulfilment.

I

LORD GIFFORD

I, Adam Gifford, sometime one of the Senators of the College of Justice, Scotland . . . I give my body to the earth as it was before, in order that the enduring blocks and materials thereof may be employed in new combinations; and I give my soul to God, in Whom and with Whom it always was, to be in Him and with Him for ever in closer and more conscious union. . . .

I

A Tribute to the Founder

This lectureship, with three others in the universities of Edinburgh, St Andrews, and Aberdeen, was founded as you know by the late Lord Gifford, a Scotch lawyer, who by ability, hard work and self-denial had amassed a large fortune, and attained the dignified position of a seat on the bench.

I have not been able to gather from his friends much information about his personal character and the private circumstances of his life. Nor do they all agree in the estimate they formed of him. Some represented him to me as a keen, hardworking, and judicious man, engrossed by his professional work, yet with a yearning for quietness, for some hours of idleness that should allow him to meditate on the great problems of life. . . . Some of his relations and a few of his more intimate friends seem to have been startled at times by the fervour and earnestness with which he spoke to them on religious and philosophical topics. Even when he was in full practice as a lawyer, the first thing he did, I am told, when he returned from the Parliament House on Saturdays, was to lock the door of his library, and devote himself to his own favourite authors, never looking at a professional book or paper till it was necessary to begin work on Monday. He had a separate set of books altogether in his bedroom, amongst which he spent every moment of his spare time during session, and probably almost his whole vacation. He was devoted to Plato as well as to Spinoza, and read philosophy both ancient and modern in all directions, as well as poetry and the best current literature of the day.

But the world at large knew him chiefly as a successful lawyer, as a man always ready to help in any useful and charitable work, and satisfied to accept the traditional forms of public worship, as a necessary tribute which every member of a religious as well as of a political community must pay for the maintenance of order, peace, and charity. During the last seven years of his life, when confined to the sick-room by creeping paralysis, his mind, always active, bright, and serene, became more and more absorbed in the study of the various systems of philosophy and religion, both Christian and non-Christian, and he made no secret to his own relatives of his having been led by these studies to surrender some of the opinions which they and he himself had been brought up to consider as essential to Christianity. There can be no doubt that he deliberately rejected all miracles, whether as a judge, on account of want of evidence, or as a Christian, because they seemed to him in open conflict with the exalted spirit of Christ's own teaching. Yet he remained always a truly devout Christian, trusting more in the great miracle of Christ's life and teaching on earth than in the small miracles ascribed to him by many of his followers.

FRIEDRICH MAX MULLER, Glasgow, 1888-92, *Natural Religion*, pp. 1-3.

2

Lectures by Adam Gifford

It is a handsome little volume; and it came to me, bound as it is, unexpectedly and with surprise, from Frankfurt-am-Main. It has, somehow, a singularly simple, pure, and taking title-page, the words on which are these: 'Lectures Delivered on Various Occasions by Adam Gifford, one of the Senators of the College of Justice, Scotland.' This title-page is followed by a perfectly correpondent modest little note, to the effect, that the lectures concerned are 'a selection from a miscellaneous number of others given from time to time by request, on very various occasions, and to greatly differing audiences, the preparation of which was a great pleasure to the lecturer', and, if 'of necessity sometimes hurried, never careless'. 'They were in no case,' it is added, 'meant for publication, and we print a few of them now only for his friends.' The signatures to that note—the 'we'—are Alice Raleigh and Herbert James Gifford; the one the niece, so long, in loving attention, associated with Lord Gifford, and the other his son. . . . There are seven of these lectures of Lord Gifford's, and they are respectively named as they come: (1) Ralph Waldo Emerson; (2) Attention as an Instrument of Self-Culture; (3) Saint Bernard of Clairvaux; (4) Substance: A Metaphysical Thought; (5) Law a Schoolmaster, or the Educational Function of Jurisprudence; (6) The Ten Avatars of Vishnu; and (7) The Two Fountains of Jurisprudence. Only two of them, then, so far as the titles would seem to suggest, belong to the writer's own profession of law, while the rest are literary, philosophical, or even metaphysical. Three of them in spirit, and even more or less in matter, might not unreasonably be held to have a direct bearing on the very

24

subject which it has been his will that the four universities of Scotland should be bound in perpetuity expressly to discuss.

What strikes one at first in these lectures, and from the very face of them, is the constant vivid writing, the literary accomplishment that everywhere obtains in them. He says once, for example, 'If first principles have not been carried out, if on the firm foundations the walls have not risen rightly, by truest plummet perpendicular towards heaven, and by bedded block parallel to the horizon; then be sure that sooner or later we must begin again, for Nature will find out our failure, and *with her there is no forgiveness.*' Surely that last is what is usually described as a *fine thought*; and there is concrete reflection throughout as well as felicitous phrase. It is in the same way that He says once: 'The prophet can *tell* his vision, but he cannot give his own *anointed* eye.'

In the lecture on Substance, naturally, we are in presence of the archpantheist, named and described by Lord Gifford as 'Benedictus de Spinoza, one of the most eminent of the philosophers who have treated of substance'. Of him, one cannot fail to see, on the part of Lord Gifford, an even familiar knowledge. If *substance* was to Spinoza God, it is no less divine to Lord Gifford; for to him God is the all-pervading substantiality and the single soul that is alone persent everywhere. Of animals, he says, 'Their mainspring is the Eternal, and every wheel and every pinion is guided by the Infinite—and there can be but *one Infinite*—this is the root-thought of the fetichism of the Indian or of the Hottentot; and this is what the Egyptian felt when he saw sacredness in the crocodile, in the ibis, or in the beetle. Said I not,' (Lord Gifford exclaims) 'said I not that the word *substance* was perhaps the grandest word in any language? There can be none grander. It is the true name of *God*. Do you not feel with me that it is almost profane to apply the word *Substance* to anything short of God? God must be the very substance and essence of the *human soul*. The human soul is neither selfderived nor self-subsisting. It did not make itself. It cannot exist alone. It is but a manifestation, a phenomenon. It would vanish if it had not a substance, and its substance is God. But if God be the *substance* of all forces and powers and of all beings, then He must be the only substance in the universe or in all possible universes. This is the grand truth on which the system of Spinoza is founded, and his whole works are simply drawing deductions therefrom.'

JAMES HUTCHISON STIRLING, Edinburgh, 1888-90, *Philosophy and Theology*, pp. 197-9, 206-7.

II

NATURAL THEOLOGY IN THE WIDEST SENSE

Therefore, I direct and appoint my said trustees . . . to pay the following sums . . . for the purpose of establishing in each of the four cities of Edinburgh, Glasgow, Aberdeen, and St Andrews, a Lectureship or Regular Chair for 'Promoting, Advancing, Teaching and Diffusing the Study of Natural Theology, in the widest sense of that term'.

3

The Task

One function of philosophy is to think dispassionately about religion.

HERBERT JAMES PATON, St Andrews, 1949-50, *The Modern Predicament*, p. 19.   .

4

The Main Business of Natural Theology

Its main business, as I understand it, is to consider how much of certain or probable knowledge is obtainable, on grounds which approve themselves to reason, concerning the existence of God; and, in the event of an affirmative answer to the question of God's existence, concerning His nature, and His relationship to the human soul. Formulated in more rough and ready, but not, I think, fundamentally misleading fashion, Natural Theology seeks a rational answer to the question 'Is religion true? And if so, in what precise sense?'

CHARLES ARTHUR CAMPBELL, St Andrews, 1953-5, *On Selfhood and Godhood*, p. 5.

5

Construing Religion

If it be said that it is the object of philosophy to construe religion, that does not mean, as sometimes seems to be supposed, that it has to construct it. To construe a thing is to set it in its relation to other things, to give it its place in a system, to deprive it of its mere individuality, and to understand its place and value. As has been said, some such appreciation or estimate is always made: but it may be made stealthily, blindly, and without due sense of proportions. The whole claim made by philosophy is that such evaluation of the factors of life shall be made consciously and with due care, and not at haphazard. It may be maintained, indeed, that, as a matter of fact, the most prominent and widespread forms of religion have grown up in a soil thoroughly saturated by philosophic influences. This is certainly true of Christianity and Buddhism. But, apart from this, we must distinguish between philosophy as a life, and philosophy as logic. In reference to life, philosophy is only instrumental and subordinate. It is the extension and deepening of intelligence; the translation, it may be said, of the *is* into the *is known*; the organization of the fragments of life—so at first they appear—into the complete structure which they really presuppose.

WILLIAM WALLACE, Glasgow, 1893-4, *Lectures and Essays on Natural Theology and Ethics*, pp. 18-19.

6

Sympathetic Criticism

Criticism must be sympathetic, or it will completely miss the mark; but it must also be dispassionate and relentless, and nothing whatever must be allowed to escape its universal inquisition. In the sciences this criticism is part of the scientific process itself; in the aesthetic sphere it has the name of criticism as used in the specialized sense; in relation to Religion the task of criticism is discharged by Natural Theology. Natural Theology should be the criticism of actual Religion and of actual religious beliefs, irrespective of their supposed origin and therefore independently of any supposed act or word of Divine Revelation, conducted with a full understanding of what is criticized, yet with the complete relentlessness of scientific enquiry.

WILLIAM TEMPLE, Glasgow, 1932-4, *Nature, Man and God*, p. 27.

7
Linguistic Analysis, 1888

A study of language is absolutely necessary as an introduction to the study of philosophy as well as of religion. Whatever further research may teach us about the true nature of language, it is clear, from a purely practical point of view, that language supplies at least the tools of thought, and that a knowledge of these tools is as essential to a philosopher, as a knowledge of his ship and his oars is to a sailor. The science of language . . . is pre-eminently an analytical science. We take languages as we find them, we trace them back to their earliest forms, and classify them, and then analyse every word till we arrive at elements which resist further analysis. These elements we call roots, and leave them for the present, as ultimate facts. In tracing the upward growth of words we arrive at a stage where we can clearly see the branching off of a large number of meanings, springing from the same stem. And among these earliest ramifications we meet with a number of names familiar to us from what is called the mythology of ancient nations. We soon discover that these mythological expressions are by no means restricted to religious ideas, but that there is a period in the growth of language in which everything may or must assume a mythological expression.

FRIEDRICH MAX MULLER, Glasgow, 1888-92, *Natural Religion*, p. 21.

8
Theologia Naturalis

Whenever we speak of the beginnings of European philosophy we think of the Greeks; and any attempt to trace the origins of natural or philosophical theology must likewise begin with them. The idea of *theologia naturalis* has come to our world from a work that has long since become classical for the Christian occident—the *De civitate Dei* of St Augustine. After attacking belief in heathen gods as an illusion throughout his first five books, he proceeds in the sixth to expound the Christian doctrine of the One God and sets out to demonstrate its thorough accordance with the deepest insights of Greek philosophy. The view of Christian theology as confirming and rounding out the truths of pre-Christian thought expresses very well the positive side of the relations between the new religion and pagan antiquity. Now for St Augustine, as for any typical Neoplatonist of his century, the one supreme representative of Greek philosophy was Plato; the other thinkers were merely minor figures around the base of Plato's mighty monument. During the Middle Ages this commanding position was gradually usurped by Aristotle, and it is only since the Renaissance that Plato has again been his serious competitor. But throughout this period Greek philosophy—whether Platonic or Aristotelian—together with a gradually increasing amount of Greek science in Latin translation, was all that was left of Greek culture in the West at a time when the knowledge of the Greek language had vanished in the general cultural decline. If the continuity of the ancient Greek tradition was never entirely broken in Europe, it is due to the fact that Greek philosophy kept it alive. But this would not have been possible had not that same philosophy, as *theologia naturalis*, served as the basis for the *theologia supernaturalis* of Christianity.

WERNER JAEGER, St Andrews, 1936, *The Theology of the Early Greek Philosophers*, pp. 1-2.

9

Natural Theology

When we speak of natural science, we do not mean the science that comes natural to us: we mean the science of nature. So too natural theology was originally the theology of nature—the theology based, not on the book of Holy Scripture, but on the book of nature, and in particular on the evidence of God's purpose in the physical world. That is to say it was traditionally concerned with what is known as the argument from design. From a scientific study of the order and purpose in the world human reason was supposed to pass to knowledge of the existence and attributes of a Creator who orders all things in accordance with a divine purpose; and that purpose was not uncommonly believed to be the welfare of man.

In this narrow sense natural theology—sometimes known also by the more grandiose term 'physicotheology'—was limited in scope: it tended to despise the more abstract traditional arguments for the existence of God and prided itself on close contact with the new facts revealed by science. One of its earliest exponents, Raymond de Sabunde, who published his *Theologia Naturalis* in 1438, regarded it as an infallible science which, as he said, 'anyone can acquire in a month and without labour'. In the long line of his successors, which runs from Francis Bacon to Paley, we find men influenced by the new empirical sciences and seeking to derive from them some support for religion. Because of its concern with the details of God's purpose in the world, natural theology tended to break up into a series of minor theologies, each studying the manifestations of divine purpose in a particular field. These subordinate theologies—which are said to have been zealously cultivated by the English—were given impressive names. Thus astrotheology studied God's purpose in the stars; hydrotheology His purpose in water; ornithotheology His purpose in birds; and so on. Treatises were composed on the religious lessons to be learned from snow, thunder, insects, locusts, bees, fishes, shell-fish, and earthquakes. These edifying works are no longer read. Perhaps we may presume, even without reading them, that they contributed little of permanent value to the cause they espoused. They serve to remind us that natural theology may become highly artificial.

HERBERT JAMES PATON, St Andrews, 1950-1, *The Modern Predicament*, pp. 20-21.

10

An Avowed Opponent of All Natural Theology

I certainly see—with astonishment—that such a science as Lord Gifford had in mind does exist. I am convinced that so far as it has existed and still exists, it owes its existence to a radical error. How then should I be in a position to further and to spread it? . . .

In the summer of 1935, after I had received the honour of being

C

invited to give these lectures, I expressly reminded the Senatus of this University of the fact that 'I am an avowed opponent of all natural theology'. Since this invitation was none the less sustained and a part of the responsibility for the resulting situation has been taken from me, I would like briefly to explain in what sense I propose to bear my share of this responsibility and to satisfy the duty of good faith toward the will of the testator, since I have accepted this invitation.

I do not know anything which could prevent me from doing justice at least *indirectly* to his intentions. 'Natural Theology' is thrown into relief by the dark background of a totally different theology. It is openly or secretly conducting a *discussion* with this other theology. It exists in *antithesis* to this theology and, as the will of Lord Gifford itself, clearly shows, it has its whole *emotional appeal* in its antithesis to this other theology. 'Natural Theology' has to make itself known, demonstrate itself and maintain itself over against this other theology by distinguishing itself from it and protecting against it. How could it do otherwise? It has at any rate never done otherwise with vigour and success. When 'Natural Theology' has this opponent no longer in view, it is notorious how soon it tends to become arid and listless. And when its conflict with this adversary no longer attracts attention, it is also notorious that interest too in 'Natural Theology' soon tends to flag. Why then should the service not be rendered it of presenting to it once more this its indispensable opponent, since the requirement is that 'Natural Theology' shall here be served? And this opponent is that totally different theology by which 'Natural Theology' lives, in so far as it must affirm what the other denies and deny what the other affirms. I could well imagine that there could be nothing more animating and stimulating for all wholehearted and halfhearted friends of 'Natural Theology' than to listen to this totally different theology once again. I could well imagine that by gaining a hearing for the voice of this totally different theology, to the best of my ability and understanding, I may actually win new friends and new sympathy for 'Natural Theology' in all spheres of society. I could well imagine that all those who do not know that ordinance which prevents me from devoting myself to 'Natural Theology' will, on hearing my lectures, feel themselves confirmed in their intention to devote themselves for their part all the more to 'Natural Theology'. But however that may be, it can only be to the good of 'Natural Theology' to be able once again to measure itself as the truth—if it is the truth!—by that which from its point of view is the greatest of errors.

KARL BARTH, Aberdeen, 1937-8, *The Knowledge of God and the Service of God*, pp. 5-7.

The Risks of Reason

It seems as if religious faith must seek reason, as a condition of its own life: and yet that, in seeking reason, it seeks its own destruction. It must seek reason: for it is impossible that any real faith can live without attempting to understand itself or develop its own intellectual content; and when it has once entered upon its course, it cannot stop short of the end. If it appeals to reason, to reason it must go. And if at any point it becomes apprehensive, and endeavours to put a stop to the process of reflection and criticism, above all if it calls in the aid of scepticism to defend itself against such criticism, it loses something of its sincerity, its wholeness of heart, and of the courage and freedom that goes only with such sincerity. Thus it is driven back upon itself and deprived of that firm hold upon thought and life which it formerly possessed. The result is that religion, which should be the great principle of unity in human life, becomes a source of the most unhappy of all its divisions. Or if, again, the other alternative be adopted, and it is recognized that, in an age of science, religion, like everything else, must submit to criticism on pain of losing its moral influence, it seems as if, at the best, we were inviting such an idealistic re-interpretation of Christianity as has been attempted by Kant, by Schelling, and by Hegel: and then, it is alleged by many, we are substituting for a religion of the heart and will, a religion of the intellect that dissolves away all those personal relations of God and man which constitute the living power of Christianity.

EDWARD CAIRD, Glasgow, 1900-02, *The Evolution of Theology in the Greek Philosophers*, Vol. 1, pp. 14-15.

12

The Spirit of Mediaeval Philosophy

The debt of the Middle Ages to the Greeks was immense, and is fully recognized, but the debt of Hellenism to the Middle Ages is as great, and nothing is less appreciated; for even from medieval religion

Greek philosophy had something to learn. Christianity communicated to it some share in its own vitality and enabled it to enter on a new career. . . .

What, then, remains in the attitude of the medieval masters to offend or embarrass us? Probably nothing save their docile modesty in instructing themselves in philosophy before setting out to further its progress. If that is a crime then they are certainly guilty, and there is no remedy left. They believed that philosophy could not possibly be the work of a single man, no matter what his genius might be, but that it progresses, like science, slowly, as the result of the patient collaboration of generations, each leaning on its predecessors in order to surpass their achievement. 'We are like dwarfs,' said Bernard of Chartres, 'seated on the shoulders of giants. We see more things than the Ancients and things more distant, but it is due neither to the sharpness of our sight nor the greatness of our stature, it is simply because they have lent us their own.' This proud modesty we have lost. Many of our contemporaries prefer to remain on the ground; they put their pride in seeing nothing at all unless they can see it by their own efforts, and console themselves for their petty stature by recollecting their advanced age. It is a sad old age that loses all its memories. If it were true, as some have said, that St Thomas was a child and Descartes a man, we, for our part, must be very near decrepitude. Let us rather hope that truth in its eternal youth shall keep our minds always young and fresh, full of hope for the future and of force to enter there.

ETIENNE GILSON, Aberdeen, 1931-2, *The Spirit of Medieval Philosophy*, pp. 425-6.

13

Argument from Design

If beauty is to retain its worth, it must be the product of design, and behind the delight in beauty there must lurk, however vaguely, the consciousness of a designer. When we are dealing with an ordinary work of art, the designer is, of course, the artist; and we are again faced with the problem how, on the naturalistic hypothesis, a chance variation like artistic genius, without survival value, happens to play so large a part

36

in the higher life of the race. But if this be true of the beauty born of human effort, how stands the case with the beauty given us by Nature? Here there can obviously be no question of art or of artists. What we admire, what we admire indeed with a passionate admiration, is, according to naturalism, but the superficial aspect of matter casually arranged. Hurrying rivers, autumnal woods, gleams of sunshine on misty crags, the sea, the clouds, and all the rest of Nature's pageant are, on this theory, the accidental effects of molecules accidentally combined, and thereafter brought into accidental relation with human sensibilities, themselves, as organs for the apprehension of beauty, accidentally evolved. If such a theory leaves us unsatisfied we can hardly supplement its unrelieved materialism by reviving the nymphs of fountain and forest, the fairies of moor and dell. It must, I venture to suggest be Theism or nothing, and of the two it must be Theism; for all these higher values manifestly press forward, each in its own way, to completion in God. As in God they must have their root if their values are to survive, so in God they must find their consummation if their promise is to be fulfilled. For Nature, limited by naturalism, can find for them neither a beginning nor an end which is adequate to their true reality.

ARTHUR JAMES BALFOUR, Glasgow, 1922-3, *Theism and Thought*, pp. 31-32.

14

How Good is the Design?

Sir Isaac Newton concludes his famous *Principia* with a general scholium, in which he maintains that 'the whole diversity of natural things can have arisen from nothing but the ideas and the will of one necessarily existing being, who is always and everywhere, God Supreme, infinite, omnipotent, omniscient, absolutely perfect'. A little more than a hundred years later Laplace began to publish his *Mécanique Céleste*, which may be described as an extension of Newton's *Principia* on Newton's lines, translated into the language of the differential calculus. When Laplace went to make a formal presentation of his work to Napoleon, the latter remarked: 'M. Laplace, they tell me you have written this large book on the system of the universe and have never even mentioned its Creator.' Whereupon Laplace drew himself up and answered bluntly: 'Sire, I had no need of any such hypothesis.' . . . Think again of the remarkable instances of special contrivance and design collected by Paley in his *Natural Theology*, published at the beginning of this century, or of those of the *Bridgewater Treatises* a generation later—works from which some of us perhaps got our first knowledge of science. Nobody reads these books now, and nobody writes others like them. Such arguments have ceased to be edifying, or even safe, since they cut both ways, as the formidable array of facts capable of an equally cogent dysteleological application sufficiently shews. But, in truth, special adaptations have ceased to lie on the confines of science, where natural causes end. 'Sturmius,' says Paley, 'held that the examination of the eye was a cure for atheism.' Yet Helmholtz, who knew incomparably more about the eye than half a dozen Sturms, describes it as an instrument that a scientific optician would be ashamed to make: and Helmholtz was no atheist.

JAMES WARD, Aberdeen, 1896-8, *Naturalism and Agnosticism*, Vol. 1, pp. 3-4, 6-7.

15

God the Artist

If we turn from the exact sciences to the field of Art, we perceive at once an interesting difference. We should never say that any competent musician or man of letters could see how a symphony of Beethoven or a play of Shakespeare should be completed, if only he had the earlier movements or acts before him. On the other hand, we do not regard this fact as meaning no more than that the composer or poet may do as he likes, and that he might have finished off his work in half a dozen ways as well as in that upon which he actually hit. On the contrary, we are disposed when we see how it is done to say 'That is the only possible way in which it could satisfactorily have been done.' Reason, the common Reason, could not anticipate but can endorse it, and can say, as Albert Dürer is reported to have said of a picture of his own, 'Sir, it could not have been better done.' In the creative activity of the artist we seem to see Personality and Reason no longer contrasted but reconciled and at one. God, it was said of old, plays the geometer; but does he not play the artist too? Or rather, is not the artist made in his image as well as the geometer and the moralist? And was not the writer of Genesis happily inspired when he imagined the Creator, like a greater Dürer, beholding 'all that he had made, and behold it was very good'?

CLEMENT CHARLES JULIAN WEBB, Aberdeen, 1918-19, *God and Personality*, pp. 268-9.

16

Thinking and Being

The agreement of our thinking with the being of the world rests on the fact that it is the reproduction of the creative thought of the Infinite mind, a reproduction which is always imperfect according to the measure of the finite mind. The truth of our cognition is a participating in *the* truth which God essentially is.

This is the proper sense and the abiding truth contained in the so-called 'Ontological Argument', the tenor of which refers to the relation of thinking and being so understood. The argument is as old as religious reflection. It is already contained in the words of the Psalmist, 'In Thy light we see light'. It forms the hinge of the philosophy of Plato, according to which the highest Idea, or God, is the ground both of knowing and of being, and all true cognition is a participation in the world of the Ideas of the Divine reason. In like manner, according to Augustine, God is the eternal truth, the ground and goal of all the true thinking of man. According to Thomas Aquinas, we see and judge all things in the light of God, in so far as the natural light of our reason is a participating in the Divine light. In the hands of Anselm this thought, which is distinctly found exhibited in his *Proslogium*, received the unfortunate scholastic turn, that from the conception of God as the most perfect Being, an inference is drawn to His existence as one of the attributes contained in the conception. This inference, which is also found repeated by Descartes and Wolff, has been rightly disposed of by Kant as a piece of school wit; but his criticism shot beyond the mark

39

and overlooked the deeper correct thought, which is concealed under the deceptive scholastic form of the ontological argument. Kant, in setting up such an opposition between Thinking and Being as that no way led from the former to the latter at all, makes not merely the Being of God, but likewise that of the world unknowable. Knowledge being separated from Being, is limited to mere subjective phenomena, and is consequently at bottom robbed of all truth.

OTTO PFLEIDERER, Edinburgh, 1894, *Philosophy and Development of Religion*, Vol. 1, pp. 146-7.

17

All Systems are Incomplete

Every system that deserves to be described as a constructive philosophy —be it dogmatic, critical, enpirical, idealist, what you will—conceives itself not merely to be rooted in reason, but to be rationalized throughout. The conceptions with which it works should be sifted, clarified, defined. It should assume nothing which requires proof. It should rest nothing (in the last resort) on faith or probability. It should admit no inexplicable residues.

Philosophers seem to me entirely right if they think that this is what a system ought to be; but not entirely right if they think that this is what any system is, or has ever been. In any case, no description could be less applicable to the point of view which I am provisionally recommending. The philosopher refuses—in theory—to assume anything that requires proof. I assume (among other things) the common-sense outlook upon life, and the whole body of the sciences. The philosopher admits—in theory—no ground of knowledge but reason. I recognize that, in fact, the whole human race, including the philosopher himself, lives by faith alone. The philosopher asks what creed reason requires him to accept. I ask on what terms the creed which is in fact accepted can most reasonably be held. The philosopher conceives that within the unchanging limits of his system an appropriate niche can be found for every new discovery as it arises. My view is that the contents of a system are always reacting on its fundamental principles, so that no philosophy can flatter itself that it will not be altered out of all recognition as knowledge grows.

ARTHUR JAMES BALFOUR, Glasgow, 1914, *Theism and Humanism*, pp. 262-3.

18

Some Conclusions

If it be objected that natural theology has had its day and is admitted on all hands to be a very inadequate foundation for any considerable theistic structure, I should have to repeat what I have often said by way of reply. In the first place, even if natural theology be insufficient of itself to prove very much, it may appreciably clarify much in theology. That would be true even if we accepted Hume's sinister comment that 'the errors in religion are dangerous, those in philosophy only ridiculous'. In the second place it is dangerous to assume that a policy that has been generally abandoned should be abandoned for ever. Rejuvenation is possible. Thirdly, and most importantly, there is the danger that arguments that were once very carefully pondered are revived unwittingly in a weaker form and treated with the reverence that is accorded to youth. In that case the level of argument sinks appreciably.

I have assumed throughout these lectures that a reasonable man may be a theist, and that he may support his theism, very largely, on grounds of common reason. The course of this enquiry, so far from having shattered that assumption, seems to me to have confirmed it. Theistic metaphysics—and theism is essentially metaphysical—is one of the great types of metaphysics, and is likely to remain so. It has been elaborated with so much ability by so many theologians and philosophers of the highest intellectual calibre that criticism has no excuse for shooting indiscriminately into the fog. The critics have a very plain target. They ought to be able to know when they hit it; but in that they may often be over-confident.

For myself I may say that I did not appreciate the force of theism when I began this enquiry. I was comforted by the recollection that Lord Gifford expressly permitted a lecturer on his foundation to be a sceptic and freethinker. I hoped to be able to avoid pulpit theism and soap-box atheism. (I may add the irrelevance that I dislike both.) I may even have thought that theism was a decrepit metaphysical vehicle harnessed to poetry. I do not think so now. While I do not think that any theistic argument is conclusive, and am of opinion that very few theistic proofs establish a high degree of probability, I also incline to the belief that theistic metaphysics is stronger than most, and that metaphysics is not at all weak in principle despite the strain that it puts upon the human intellect. It is quite impossible, I believe, to refute theism. A verdict of 'not proven' is easier to obtain, largely because proof is so difficult and its standards so exacting. If plausibility were enough, theism is much more plausible than most other metaphysical conclusions.

JOHN LAIRD, Glasgow, 1939-40, *Mind and Deity*, pp. 318-20.

19

Drop the Term?

The term 'natural theology', then, has been used in the four different ways. . . . The first usage—to indicate the attempt to construct any sort of world-view, though more particularly perhaps one of a broadly idealist kind—we can obviously set on one side; it is strained and unfamiliar, and there are better ways of describing what is in mind. The second usage—to indicate the attempt to establish theism by demonstrative, rational *a priori* argument—may also be set on one side. If we want a name for it we can follow Tennant and call it rational theology. The third usage—to indicate the attempt to present theism as a reasonable and satisfying (indeed, the most reasonable and satisfying), though not logically demonstrative, world-view—seems to me to be the most satisfactory. . . . The fourth usage, which makes natural theology equivalent to natural religion, or, alternatively, to the theistic beliefs which are implicit in, arise out of, and are sustained by a spontaneous religious response to the world (reflective elements not necessarily being absent), is obviously confusing. . . .

Can the attempt to build a Christian theistic world-view be properly brought under the rubric of 'natural theology'? It must be admitted that such a use of the term seems extremely odd; nevertheless, in the light of the line of thought we have followed it certainly loses some of its apparent oddness. If *any* attempt to formulate a theistic world-view rests on prior insights and convictions, and if, as we have argued, there is reason to call any such attempt 'natural theology', there would appear to be no reason why the attempt to formulate a theism on the basis of certain specifically Christian insights and convictions should not be called 'natural theology' also, provided only, as I have said, nothing is introduced in a merely authoritarian and overriding way and regarded as outside the scope of critical examination. But perhaps the proper issue of the whole discussion, as I have long been inclined to think . . . would be to drop the term 'natural theology' altogether.

HERBERT HENRY FARMER, Glasgow, 1949-50, *Revelation and Religion*, pp. 8, 19-20.

20

Keep the Term?

Just as the more physical sides of science are built up from the statistical study of the movements and interactions of molecules, atoms and smaller particles, so ecology and ethology are using the scientific method by recording in quantitative terms the behaviour of animals as living wholes without necessarily adopting the dogma of materialism. Psychology is a science in the same way: a science of human behaviour, but not, I believe, in the sense of the so-called 'behaviourists'. The natural theology that I envisage is a science of the same kind: a science of man's religious behaviour. More than a hundred years ago Archbishop Frederick Temple, before natural theology had fallen into disrepute among leaders of the church, saw that this change must come.

Our theology (he wrote) has been cast in a scholastic mould, i.e. all based on logic. We are in need of, and we are being gradually forced into a theology based on psychology. The transition, I fear, will not be without much pain; but nothing can prevent it.

Just as ecology and ethology have become branches of true science because the earlier naturalists prepared the way by collecting a vast array of facts and observations, so, I believe, our future science of theology must be built upon an enormous collection of observations regarding man's religious experience and behaviour.

ALISTER HARDY, Aberdeen, 1963-5, *The Divine Flame*, pp. 219-20.

43

III
MAN'S CONCEPTIONS
OF GOD

They may freely discuss (and it may be well to do so) all questions about man's conceptions of God or the Infinite, their origin, nature, and truth, whether he can have such conceptions . . . and so on.

The Evidence of Anthropology

We meet, among the most backward peoples known to us, among men just emerged from the paleolithic stage of culture, men who are involved in dread of ghosts, a religious Idea which certainly is not born of ghost-worship, for by these men, ancestral ghosts are not worshipped. In their hearts, on their lips, in their moral training we find (however blended with barbarous absurdities, and obscured by rites of another origin) the faith in a Being who created or constructed the world; who was from time beyond memory or conjecture; who is eternal, who makes for righteousness, and who loves mankind. This Being has not the notes of degeneration; his home is 'among the stars', not in a hill or in a house. To him no altar smokes, and for him no blood is shed.

'God, that made the world and all things therein, seeing that He is lord of heaven and earth, dwelleth not in temples made with hands; neither is worshipped with men's hands, as though He needed any-thing . . . and hath made of one blood all nations of men . . . that they should seek the Lord, if haply they might feel after Him, and find Him, though He be not far from every one of us: for in Him we live, and move, and have our being.'

That the words of St Paul are literally true, as to the feeling after a God who needs not anything at man's hands, the study of anthropology seems to us to demonstrate.

ANDREW LANG, St Andrews, 1888-90, *The Making of Religion*, p. 292.

The Theology of Simple Folk

I am aware that the description of beliefs and customs which the enlightened portion of mankind has long agreed to dismiss as false

and absurd, if not as monstrous, vicious, and cruel, is apt to be somewhat tedious and repellent. . . . Still I trust that an account even of
crude theories and preposterous practices may not be wholly destitute
of interest and instruction, if it enables us to picture to ourselves
something of the effort which it has cost our predecessors to grope
their way through the mists of ignorance and superstition to what passes
with us of this generation for the light of knowledge and wisdom.
They were the pioneers who hewed their way through a jungle that
might well have seemed impenetrable to man: they made the paths
smooth for those who were to come after: we walk in their footsteps,
and reap at our ease the harvest which they sowed with labour and
anguish. The gratitude we owe them for the inestimable service which
they have rendered us should temper the harsh judgments which we
are too apt to pass on their errors, on what a hasty verdict stigmatizes
as their follies and their crimes; and the lesson which we draw from the
contemplation of their long wanderings and manifold aberrations in
the search of the true and the good should be one rather of humility
than of pride; it should teach us how weak and frail is human nature,
and by what a slender thread hangs the very existence of our species,
like a speck or mote suspended in the inconceivable infinities of the
universe.

Accordingly, the natural theology which I propose to treat is the
theology of simple folk, not the theology of the schools, where the
doctrine of the divine nature has been elaborated and refined by age-
long discussion and the successive contributions of generations of
subtle thinkers.

JAMES GEORGE FRAZER, Edinburgh, 1924-5, *The Worship of
Nature*, Vol. I, pp. 13-14.

23

They Say that God Lives Very High

The Pare Mountains form a range running southward from Mount
Kilimanjaro, near the eastern boundary of Tanganyika Territory. The
greater part of the mountains is inhabited by a tribe called the Wapare
or Wasu. Among them have been recorded some ancient and half-

forgotten legends of a good God, the Creator of the world, whom they called Kyumbi. They say that he gave their forefathers cattle, in order that they might clothe themselves in the hides, for he pitied their nakedness. He gave them also maize and the fruits of the field, and taught them to till the ground, for they suffered from hunger. God was near, men lived in communion with him. But Kiriamagi, the Eater of Eggs, the Deceiver, the Serpent, tempted men to eat eggs, which Kyumbi had forbidden them to do. And God punished them with a great famine, so that they began to eat beetles in order to save their lives. All mankind died, except two, a young man and a young woman. From them all the generations of the earth are descended. Now God was still near to men. But when men multiplied they grew froward, and they spake among themselves, saying, 'Come, let us build a tower, whose top shall reach to the upper land, in order that we may creep up it and wage war on Him that is above in His own country.' But Kyumbi looked down on them as a man looks down on a heap of ants, and he said, 'What are these little pigmies down below there?' Then the earth quaked, and the tower broke in two, and buried the builders under the ruins. But Kyumbi moved the upper land far away, and ever since he has not been near men, but far, far away. And since that day men have sought God, and wished to draw him down to them, but they could not; for Kyumbi hearkened to them no more.

JAMES GEORGE FRAZER, Edinburgh, 1924-5, *The Worship of Nature*, Vol. 1, pp. 200-201.

24

Self-conscious Man

Religion, however, is not really like a machine into which one puts in raw instinct at one end so as to turn out a finished morality at the other. Essentially it is a mode of living. Moreover, it is a mode belonging to that higher grade of living when the directive principle, which throughout is self-determining, is becoming self-conscious. That this advance in self-consciousness is on the whole beneficial to the species may be taken as a biological axiom; the presumption likewise being that it somehow affects the directive principle for the better. In other words, our powers of self-guidance may be supposed to improve if, and in so far as, we can achieve self-knowledge. Yet whether we can ever come to know ourselves completely is highly doubtful. . . Religion, then, as an activity of the self-conscious or reflective type has to content itself with imaging, or symbolically expressing, as best it can, something within and yet beyond consciousness, something not wholly given because at the same time giving, namely, the life-feeling itself, the concentrated thrust of the racial instincts. The other animals just live; but man has superfluous energy enough to say to himself as he lives, 'Here I am living!' and somehow it helps him to live better. By a tortuous effort of mental gymnastics he pats himself on his own back and is greatly cheered.

ROBERT RANULPH MARETT, St Andrews, 1931-2, *Faith, Hope and Charity in Primitive Religion*, pp. 30-1.

25

Plato's God

If the Good is the sole cause of Being, it will follow . . . that the whole of Nature, so far as it really exists, is a revelation of God. This is the thought which Plato endeavours to work out in the *Timaeus*, where he represents the world as a divine child, the 'image of its maker, a perceivable God, most mighty and good, most beautiful and perfect'. The Creator, being altogether free from envy, desired that everything should be made as like as possible unto himself. The student of nature is consequently a seeker after God, provided he endeavours to trace, in the phenomena which he investigates, the operation of the Good. We have seen that Socrates tried to inculcate piety by dwelling on the adaptation of nature exclusively to the needs of man. The teleology of Plato is no longer anthropocentric. He believes that each particular organism has its appointed function to perform, and is good just in proportion as it fulfils the purpose and attains the end for which it was created by the divine mind. But at the same time all these different ends conspire together for the good of the whole, which is the ultimate or perfect end. The most emphatic assertion of this thoroughly Platonic doctrine occurs in a famous passage of the *Laws*. 'The ruler of the universe has ordered all things with a view to the excellence and preservation of the whole, and each part, as far as may be, has an action and passion appropriate to it. . . . For every physician and every skilled artist does all things for the sake of the whole, directing his effort toward the common good, executing the part for the sake of the whole, and not the whole for the sake of the part.'

JAMES ADAM, Aberdeen, 1904-06, *The Religious Teachers of Greece*, pp. 448-9.

26

Aristotle's God

When we turn from Plato to Aristotle, it is usually said that we turn from the warmth of feeling to the coldness of the understanding, from the luxuriance of figurative phrase to the dryness of the technical term, from poetry to prose; but to my mind these five chapters[1] of Aristotle are, *at least in their ideas*, more poetical than anything in Plato. That πρῶτον κινοῦν of Aristotle, let certain critics find what fault they may with it, is as near as possible, as near as possible for a Greek then, the Christian God. And Aristotle *sings* Him, if less musically than Milton still in his own deep way, *musically*, and in a vastly deeper depth *philosophically* than Milton. Especially in the seventh chapter of the twelfth book it is that we find that wonderful concentration and intensity of thought, which, deep, dense, metalline-close, glows—unexpectedly and with surprise—glows into song—the psalm, the chant *de profundis*, of an Aristotle. It proceeds somewhat in this way:

As there comes not possibly anything, or all, out of night and nothingness, there must be the unmoved mover, who, in his eternity, is actual, and substantial, one. Unmoved himself, and without a strain, he is the end-aim of the universe towards which all strain. Even beauty is not moved, but moves; and we move to beauty because it is beauty, not that it is beauty only because we move to it. And the goal, the aim, the end, moves even as beauty moves, or as something that is loved moves. It is thought that has made the beginning. As mere actuality,

---

[1] *Metaphysics*, Book xii, (Λ) Chapters 6-10.

actuality pure and simple, as that which could not not-be, God knows not possibility, he is before and above and without potentiality, the beginning, the middle, and the end, the first and last, the principle and goal, without peers as without parts, immaterial, imperishable, personal, single, one, eternal and immortal. On him hang the heavens and the earth. And his joy of life is always, as is for brief moments when at its best, ours. In him indeed is that enduringly so. But it is impossible for us. For joy in him is his actuality—even as to us the greatest joy is to be awake, to see and feel, to think, and so to revive to ourselves memories and hopes. Thought, intellection is his; and his intellection is the substantial intellection of that which is substantial, the perfect intellection of that which is perfect. Thought as thought, intellection as intellection, knows itself even in apprehension of its object; for holding and knowing this, it is this, and knowing and known are identical. Intellection, indeed, takes up into itself what is to be known, and what substantially is: it acts and is the object in that it has and holds it. What, then, there is of divine in intellection, that is diviner still in its actuality in God; and speculation is what is the highest joy and the best. And if, as with us interruptedly, it is always in felicity so with God, then is there cause for wonder; and for much more wonder if the felicity with God is of a higher order than ever it is with us. But that is so. In him is life; for the actuality of intellection is life, and that actuality is his. Actuality that is absolute—*that*, as life of him, is life best and eternal. So it is we say that God is a living being, perfect and eternal. Life eternal and enduring being belong to God. And God is that.

That is a great passage.

JAMES HUTCHISON STIRLING, Edinburgh, 1888-90, *Philosophy and Theology*, pp. 139-40.

27

In the Valley of the Nile

It was given to the Egyptians to be one among the few inventive races of mankind. They were pioneers of civilization; above all they were inventors of religious ideas. The ideas, it is true, were not self-evolved;

52

they presupposed beliefs which had been bequeathed by the past; but their logical development and the forms which they assumed were the work of the Egyptian people. We owe to them the chief moulds into which religious thought has since been thrown. The doctrines of emanation, of a trinity wherein one god manifests himself in three persons, of absolute thought as the underlying and permanent substance of all things, all go back to the priestly philosophers of Egypt. Gnosticism and Alexandrianism, the speculations of Christian metaphysic and the philosophy of Hegel, have their roots in the valley of the Nile. The Egyptian thinkers themselves, indeed, never enjoyed the full fruition of the ideas they had created; their eyes were blinded by the symbolism which had guided their first efforts, their sight was dulled by overmuch reverence for the past, and the materialism which came of a contentment with this life.

ARCHIBALD HENRY SAYCE, Aberdeen, 1900-02, *The Religions of Ancient Egypt and Babylonia*, pp. 250-1.

28

By the Waters of Babylon

The exiles in Babylon would soon have been absorbed by their neighbours if they had not been kept separate by their worship of a righteous God. Many no doubt were so absorbed; but the main body held its way through much suffering, and became more and more a faithful remnant. With the third generation came a change of outlook. If they had not ceased to be victims of war, they were also witnesses for Jehovah. Even in Babylon their lofty monotheism found admirers, as it always did till Christianity outshone it. So sons of the stranger joined themselves to Jehovah, and even common men began to feel that Israel was the Servant of Jehovah, who should bring forth judgment or the knowledge of Jehovah to the Gentiles. But this made the difficulty greater than ever. Why does Israel suffer, though he is the Servant of Jehovah? Nay rather, replies the prophet, Israel suffers just because he is the Servant of Jehovah, and his sufferings are for the healing of the nations. The proselytes he has made in Babylon are no more than the first-fruits of a world of Gentiles that shall be won to the service of righteousness by the suffering of Israel. Ought not the Servant of Jehovah to have suffered these things, and to enter into his glory?

The Servant of Jehovah is Israel, but of course not Israel in his actual state of sin, for which the Servant has to make atonement. Nor does he seem to be the godly part of the nation: he is rather Israel in an ideal state personified. His kingdom is not of this world. He rules not by force but by the willing submission of the nations. His glory is not the royal glory of a Solomon, but the more than royal majesty that is won by suffering; and his redemptive work is not for the weak and ignorant only like the Law, but for the rebels and blasphemers who are beyond the mercy of the Law.

HENRY MELVILL GWATKIN, Edinburgh, 1904-05, *The Knowledge of God*, Vol 2, pp. 38-39.

29

The Roman Mind

In explaining the relation of Man to God, Cicero uses an expression which some years before he had developed in a fine passage in the Republic: *true law*, he says, *is right reason*. In the Laws he takes it up again, and argues that as both God and Man have reason, there must be a direct relation between them. And as Law and right reason are identical, we may say that Law is the binding force of that relation. And again, this means that the universe may be looked on as one great State (*civitas*), of which both God and Man (or gods and men) are citizens, or in another way as a State of which the constitution is itself the Reason, or God's law, which all reasonable beings must obey. Such obedience is itself the effort by which Man realises his own reason: he is a part of a reasonable universe, and he cannot rebel against its law without violating his own highest instinct. It is not hard to see how this way of expressing the Stoic theological principle would appeal to the Roman mind. That mind was wholly incapable of metaphysical thinking; but it could without effort understand, with the help of its social and political principles and experience, the idea of a supreme intelligent rule. . . . The idea of God in any such sense as this was indeed new to him; but he could grasp it under the expression 'universal law of right reason' when he would have utterly failed, for example, to conceive of it as 'the Absolute'. He can feel himself the citizen of a State whose maker and ruler is God, and whose law is the inevitable force of Reason; he can realize his relationships to God as a part of the same State, gifted with the same power of discerning its legal basis, nay, even helping to administer its law by rational obedience.

WILLIAM WARDE FOWLER, Edinburgh, 1909-10, *The Religious Experience of the Roman People*, pp. 370-1.

30

The Stoics

The Stoics were strong in their conception of man's sovereign place in the universe, and in their firm cheerful faith in the rationality of the cosmos. They saw and said that in the world, after God, there is nothing so important as man, and in man nothing so important as reason; that, therefore, the true theology is that which offers to faith a rational divinity, and the true life that which consists in following the dictates of reason as active in the individual and immanent in the universe. But their errors were serious. They starved and blighted human nature by finding no place or function for passion, and worshipping as their ethical ideal apathetic wisdom. They shut their eyes to patent facts of experience by pretending to regard outward events as insignificant and pain as no evil. They silenced the voice of humanity in their hearts by indulging in merciless contempt for the weak and the foolish; that is to say, for the great mass of mankind who have not mastered the art of treating pain as a trifle, and gained complete victory over passionate impulse.

ALEXANDER BALMAIN BRUCE, Glasgow, 1897-8, *The Moral Order of the World*, pp. 387-8.

55

31

The Greek Contribution to Christian Thought

In different ways Greek philosophy may be regarded as the germ out of which Christian theology sprang, or as the great adverse force which it had to combat. It was the former, if we consider that in Neo-Platonism Greek philosophy was struggling with the ideas of the antagonism between the divine and the human, and at the same time of the necessity of their relation. The problem which Christianity had to solve, reached its most definite and decisive expression in the Neo-Platonic philosophy. And we must remember that he, who puts such a problem distinctly before the human mind, has already done much to help towards its solution. On the other hand, Neo-Platonism itself was not able to reach such a solution. It set the two terms in such absolute opposition that a true synthesis or reconciliation of them was impossible. It altogether separated the Infinite from the finite; or, if it tried to mediate between them by means of the intelligence and the world-soul, yet as it regarded even the world-soul as belonging entirely to the intelligible world, it could not conceive it as descending into the world of sense and matter, or as reconciling the world of sense and matter with the divine. Its last word was escape, not reconciliation, the deliverance of the soul from the bonds of finitude, and not the conversion of the finite itself into the organ and manifestation of the infinite. Hence when brought in relation to Christianity, Neo-Platonism became an influence in favour of dualism. It tended to break the unity of life and thought which Christianity sought to establish, or at least to limit and make imperfect the reconciliation which Christianity sought to attain.

EDWARD CAIRD, Glasgow, 1900-02, *The Evolution of Theology in the Greek Philosophers*, Vol. 2, pp. 369-70.

32

Transition

The Latin peasants were—and are still—an ignorant race, tenacious of old habits and traditions. They clung to the religion of their fathers because it pleased them to know and to feel that their interests were intrusted to the never failing care of local spirits, their own personal friends as it were, and because they saw in the commonest phenomena of nature the manifestation of a superior power, springs, rivers, caves, trees, forests, hills, and mountains all appeared to those simple minds fraught with life and visible embodiments of divine agents. They divided these salutary and beneficent beings into two classes: one comprising the higher gods of nature, Apollo, Diana, Silvanus, Pan, etc.; the other restricted to local spirits, nymphs, fauns, and the 'genii loci'. . . .

It is easy to conceive what obstacles the preachers of the gospel must have found in these deeply rooted superstitions in consequence of which the Campagna remained essentially pagan long after the gods had been expelled from their temples in the City. The study of local traditions, of folklore, of the origin of many suburban sanctuaries and shrines, would help us greatly to make out how the religious transformation of the Campagna was gently brought about. . . .

The picturesque shrines which the explorer of the Campagna and of the Sabine and Volscian districts meets at the crossing of roads and lanes have not changed their site or purpose: only the crescent which once shone on the forehead of Diana the huntress is now trodden by the feet of the Virgin Mary, who also appears crushing the head of the snake once sacred to Juno Lanuvina; but the wild flowers still perfume with their delicious scent the 'iconetta', as the shrine is still called in the Byzantine fashion among our peasantry, and the sweet oil, instead of being poured over the altar, burns before the image of the Mother of God in quaint little lamps. The month of May, once sacred to the Dea Dia, has become the month of Mary.

RODOLFO AMEDIO LANCIANI, St Andrews, 1899-1900, *New Tales of Old Rome*, pp. 112, 114-15.

33

Tertullian and Bishop Butler

Two familiar and pregnant sayings, the one from an apologist of Christianity in the third century, and the other from an apologist of Christianity in the eighteenth, may well serve to indicate my point of view. Tertullian, in the Treatise *De Testimonio Animae*, which has been described, not excessively, as the most original and acute of his works, claimed for Christianity that it expressed the beliefs and aspirations of the human spirit itself. It was, in fact, natural religion *par excellence*. Thus he apostrophizes the human soul:

'Stand forth in the midst of us, O soul! I appeal to thee; yet not as wise with a wisdom formed in the schools, trained in libraries, or nourished in Attic academies and porticoes; but as simple and rough, without polish or culture, such as thou art to those who have thee only, such as thou art in the crossroad, the highway, and the dockyard. I seek of thee that which thou bringest with thee into man, that which thou hast thyself learnt to think, or hast been taught by thy Creator, Whoever He may be. Thou art not, so far as I know, Christian. The soul is not born Christian, but becomes Christian. Yet Christians beg now for a testimony from thee, as from one outside them; a testimony against thine own that the heathen may blush for their hatred and mockery of us.'[1]

Tertullian, arguing against the pagans, claimed that the human spirit is naturally Christian. Fifteen hundred years later Butler, arguing against the Deists, who were neo-Pagans in their attitude towards Christianity, maintained that Christianity is but the 'republication' of natural religion. That is the assumption on which I propose to ground the argument, that the morality which Christ's religion properly requires is precisely that which the conscience and reason of modernly civilized men approve. . . .

Thus we shall affirm the view which Bishop Butler expressed in the terms of eighteenth-century thought, *viz.* that it is only in Christianity that natural religion receives fair and full expression:

'Christianity is a republication of natural Religion. It instructs mankind in the moral system of the world: that it is the work of an infinitely perfect Being, and under His government; that virtue is His law; and that He will finally judge mankind in righteousness, and render to all according to their works, in a future state. And, which is very material, it teaches natural Religion in its genuine simplicity; free from those superstitions with which it was totally corrupted, and under which it was in a manner lost.'[2]

HERBERT HENSLEY HENSON, St Andrews, 1935-6, *Christian Morality*, pp. 2-3.

[1] *De Testimonio Animae*, cap. i.
[2] Analogy, Part ii, cap. i.

The Medieval Synthesis

The Aristotelian tradition was represented in its purest and most uncompromising form by the teaching of the Spanish Moslem Averroes (Ibn Rushd, 1126-98), whose works were translated after 1217 by Michael Scot (d. 1232), the court astrologer of Frederick II, and found enthusiastic disciples in Siger of Brabant and his followers in the University of Paris from 1270 to 1280, and at Bologna and Padua in the fourteenth century.

The result of this great influx of new knowledge was to provide the universities and the international societies of scholars and teachers who frequented them with the materials from which to construct a new intellectual synthesis. The dialecticians were no longer compelled to masticate and remasticate the old scholastic commonplaces. They had at last something solid to get their teeth into. And for a hundred years there was, in consequence, such a development of philosophical studies as the world had not seen since the great age of ancient Greece. The effect on general culture may be seen in a unique form in the *Divina Commedia* of Dante, the greatest literary achievement of the Middle Ages, in which every aspect of life and every facet of personal and historic experience is illuminated by a metaphysical vision of the universe as an intelligible unity. And behind the *Divina Commedia* there is the work of St Thomas and St Albert and a hundred lesser men, all of them devoted to the building up of a great structure of thought in which every aspect of knowledge is co-ordinated and sub-ordinated to the divine science—*Theologia*—the final transcendent end of every created intelligence.

The great interest of this synthesis is not its logical completeness, for that was to be found already in rudimentary form in the traditional curriculum of the earlier medieval schools, but rather the way in which the mind of Western Christendom reconquered the lost world of Hellenic science and annexed the alien world of Moslem thought without losing its spiritual continuity or its specifically religious values.

CHRISTOPHER DAWSON, 1947-9, *Religion and the Rise of Western Culture*, pp. 233-4.

St Thomas Aquinas

God's knowledge must of necessity extend as far as His causality extends. Now His creative virtue may properly be so called precisely because it is not limited to the transmission of forms, but gives being to matter itself. . . . Plato's gods may throw the task of regulating the lot of individuals on some general law; Aristotle's unmoved movers may be wholly uninterested in what goes on in the universe; nothing could be more natural, for neither one nor the other has created matter, and consequently need not know it. Now if they have no knowledge of matter they must inevitably be without knowledge of the beings which it individualizes. But in a universe in which all being is created, the material and the individual must of necessity fall within the grasp of the divine intelligence.

If, then, the case stands thus, providence can by no means stop short at the universal; rather we should say, as in the case of the divine ideas, that it is essentially on the particulars that it bears. But the particular is not to be divorced from the order into which it enters, the order of the work is part of the work; and therefore He Who made the world must have known, foreseen and willed what the world would be down to its least details. Nothing is more remarkable than the continuity of the tradition throughout the whole Judeo-Christian doctrine of creation. The God of the medieval philosophers remains identical with the God of the Bible, that is to say Being, the Creator, the Lord, and finally, in consequence, the Free Orderer of all things. St Thomas has synthesized the *ensemble* of these views in a page so perfect, that we cannot do better than let him present them in all the rigour of their order: 'We have shown that there is a First Being, possessing the full perfection of all being, Whom we call God, and Who also, of the abundance of His perfection, bestows being on all that exists, so that He must be recognized to be not only the first of beings, but also the first principle of beings. Now this being bestows being on others not by any necessity of His nature, but according to the decree of His will, as we have shown above. Hence it follows that He is the Lord of all things He has made, as we too are masters of those things that are subject to our will. And this dominion which He exercises over all that He has made is absolute, for since He has produced them without the help of an extrinsic agent, and even without matter as the basis of His work, He is the universal efficient cause of the totality of being. Now everything that is produced through the will of an agent is directed to an end by that agent; because the good and the end are the proper object of the will, wherefore whatever proceeds from a will must needs be directed to an end. And each thing attains its end by its action, but this action needs to be directed by Him Who endowed things with the principle whereby they act. Consequently God, Who in Himself is perfect in every way, and by His power endows all things with being, must needs be the Ruler of all, Himself ruled by none: nor is anything to be excepted from His ruling as neither is there anything that does not owe to Him its being. Therefore as He is perfect in being and causing, so also is He perfect in ruling.' The whole Augustinian metaphysic of creation is resumed in these lines, but now it has achieved a perfect consciousness of itself, comes face to face with itself in its own clear limpidity.

ETIENNE GILSON, Aberdeen, 1931-2, *The Spirit of Medieval Philosophy*, pp. 160-2.

36

The Renaissance and the Reformation

The Renaissance and Reformation represent partly contradictory historical forces, released by the disintegration of the medieval synthesis. For the Renaissance the Catholic interpretation of the human situation is too pessimistic; and for the Reformation it is too optimistic. But since the Catholic synthesis is more optimistic than pessimistic there is more affinity between the Renaissance and Catholicism than between Reformation and Renaissance or between the Reformation and Catholicism. The line between Catholic and Renaissance perfectionism is comparatively unbroken, though the Renaissance dispenses with 'grace' as a prerequisite power for the fulfilment of life. It finds the capacities for fulfilment in human life itself. The Reformation on the other hand represents a more complete break with the medieval tradition; for it interprets 'grace' primarily, not as the 'power of God' in man, but as the power (forgiveness) of God towards man. It denies that either an individual life or the whole historical enterprise can be brought to the degree of completion which Catholic theories of grace imply.

The Renaissance opposes the ecclesiastical control of all cultural life in the name of the autonomy of human reason and thereby lays the foundation for the whole modern cultural development.The Reformation opposes the dogmatic controls of religious thought by the church in the name of the authority of Scripture, insisting that no human authority (not even that of the church) can claim the right of possessing and interpreting the truth of the gospel, which stands beyond all human wisdom and which is invariably corrupted (at least in detail) by these interpretations.Each one of these protests against the church's pretended sole right or ability to interpret and to apply the final truth has its own validity.

REINHOLD NIEBUHR, Edinburgh, 1939, *The Nature and Destiny of Man*, Vol. 2, pp. 155-6.

37

Luther

To Luther, therefore, faith is at the same time these two things: the religious possession of salvation, and the moral motive of sanctification. It connects man with God, frees him from human mediators and means, and makes him immediately certain within of his salvation; but it connects him at the same time with human society, and impels him to serve men gratuitously from free love without selfish seeking of reward, and to exercise in this service of love to man his practical service of God. This is the Reformation faith in its purest religious moral sense, if we look away from the dogmatic coverings by which it is veiled, which certainly but too soon again obtrude themselves. It is the Christianity of Paul and of Augustine which we see revive again in Luther. With these two he shared the deep feeling of human sin and unfreedom and the elevating experience of the free and renovating grace of God; but in distinction from Augustine, Luther saw the divine grace, not as conjoined with the Church and its means of salvation, but only with Christ and His gospel; and hence the doctrine of grace, which in Augustine had subjected man to the slavish yoke of the Church, became in Luther rather the means of liberating him from all human dependence, and binding him to God alone. . . . When at the Leipzic disputation he was harassed by his opponent Ech with the authority of the Pope and of the Councils, he declared, 'I believe that I am a Christian theologian, and live in the kingdom of truth; and therefore I will be free and will give myself up to no authority, whether it be of a Council or of the Emperor, or of the universities or of the Pope, so that I may confidently confess all that I know as truth, whether it is asserted by a Catholic or a heretic, and whether it is accepted or rejected by a Council. Why shall I not venture the attempt, if I, one man, can point to a better authority than a Council?' . . . At least the principle of autonomous thinking, of freedom of conscience and reason, was clearly and distinctly set up by Luther from the time of the Leipzic disputation and the Diet of Worms.

OTTO PFLEIDERER, Edinburgh, 1894, *Philosophy and Development of Religion*, Vol. 2, pp. 329-31.

38

Calvin

What then is the specific nature of the religious phenomenon? All religion is based on the recognition of a superhuman Reality of which man is somehow conscious and towards which he must in some way orientate his life. The existence of the tremendous transcendent reality that we name GOD is the foundation of all religion in all ages and among all peoples.

As Calvin writes at the beginning of the *Institutes*:

'We lay it down as a position not to be controverted, that the human mind, even by natural instinct, possesses some sense of a Deity. For that no man might shelter himself under the pretext of ignorance, God hath given to all some apprehension of his existence, the memory of which he frequently and insensibly renews; so that as men universally know that there is a God, and that he is their Maker, they must be condemned by their own testimony, for not having worshipped him and consecrated their lives to his service. If we seek for ignorance of a Deity, it is nowhere more likely to be found, than among tribes the most stupid and farthest from civilization. But, as (the celebrated)

Cicero observes, there is no nation so barbarous, no race so savage, as not to be firmly persuaded of the being of a God. Even those who in other respects appear to differ but little from brutes, always retain some sense of religion, so fully are the minds of men possessed with this common principle, which is closely interwoven with their original composition. Now since there has never been a country or family, from the beginning of the world, totally destitute of religion, it is a tacit confession, that some sense of the Divinity is inscribed on every heart.'[1]

I quote the testimony of Calvin rather than that of St Thomas or St Augustine because it is with the former that we find the traditional Christian doctrine of Natural Theology reduced to a minimum. No theologian has taken a more gloomy view of the ruinous or impotent state of human nature abandoned to itself, none has been less inclined to set a value on any knowledge which man can acquire concerning the nature of God by the power of his own reason. Yet even for Calvin there is no question of the fact that the human mind possesses a natural knowledge of the existence of God which is inseparable from its very constitution—'a doctrine which has not to be learnt in schools, but of which every man is master from birth and which nature herself allows no man to forget although many strive with all their might to do so'.

In fact, whenever there is any recognition of any kind of religious truth, some place, however lowly, must always be found for Natural Theology. Its radical denial is only possible where religion is regarded as a form of mass delusion which may have had a great importance for human culture, but can have no objective truth or validity.

CHRISTOPHER DAWSON, Edinburgh, 1947-9, *Religion and Culture*, pp. 25-7.

39

The God of the Deists

Francis Bacon said that a knowledge of God obtained in this way (i.e. through reason) may suffice 'to convince atheism, but not to inform

---

[1] The Latin version of this passage has been replaced by the translation which appears in a footnote in the original work.

religion'. It is indeed remarkable how far even the deistical writers of the seventeenth and eighteenth centuries believed such knowledge could extend. According to Lord Herbert of Cherbury it extended to the propositions (1) that a Supreme Being exists, (2) that he ought to be worshipped, (3) that virtue is the principal part of his worship, (4) that faults are to be expiated by repentance, and (5) that there will be rewards and punishments in a future life. And Spinoza's list is as follows: (1) that a Supreme Being exists, (2) that he is one, (3) that he is omnipresent, all things being open to him, (4) that he has supreme right and dominion over all things, (5) that his worship consists only in justice and charity in regard to our neighbours, (6) that 'all those, and those only, who obey God by their manner of life are saved' and (7) that God forgives the sins of those who repent. Both Herbert and Spinoza describe their lists as comprising 'the dogmas of universal religion', the former contending that they are innately implanted by God in the minds of all men, and the latter that they are either thus 'written on the hearts of all men' or are reached by the use of figures provided by the prophetic imagination. But in neither case is there postulated any present activity of communication of the Spirit of God with the human spirit. Religion is an altogether one-sided thing. As is well known, Spinoza taught that 'he who loves God cannot expect that God should love him in return'.

JOHN BAILLIE, Edinburgh, 1961-2, *The Sense of the Presence of God*, p. 123.

40

God is more than a Convenient Concept

Like the exponents of other world-outlooks, the theist is recommending a conceptual scheme,which is to be used for making the facts of experience comprehensible. But he is doing more, wheher he likes it or not. He is making assertions. He does not merely propose that we make use of the *concept* of a creative and loving Supreme Being. He asserts that this concept has an instance, that there actually *is* a Supreme Being who created the world, that he actually *is* infinite in power, wisdom and goodness, and moreover that he actually *does* love every single person whom he has created. To put it in another way; in the Theistic world outlook, the idea of such a Supreme Being is not just a conceptual device, an 'auxiliary concept' to be used for facilitating certain intellectual operations.

Let us contrast it with the concept of a set of lines of latitude and longitude, which geographers invite us to use in order to render the spatial relations of various parts of the earth's surface more comprehensible. A geographer never dreams of claiming that these lines (or the grid-like structure which they form) are actually existing entities, or that they do actually embrace the earth's surface like a network of wire. They are merely conceptual devices, and when a geographer recommends us to conceive of them he is not asserting that there are any additional entities in the world, over and above those which we actually observe. But this is just what the Theist does assert. He asserts that there *is* an additional entity, over and above those which we learn about by means of sense-perception, memory and scientific and historical investigation. He is not merely proposing that we use a certain concept or set of concepts for rendering the universally admitted facts comprehensible. He asserts that there is another fact over and above these universally admitted ones, namely the fact that there is a God—a loving God—who created the world. He claims, moreover, that this is the fact upon which all the universally admitted ones depend, and that it alone renders them comprehensible. This is the sense in which this world-outlook is not a purely immanent one.

HENRY HABBERLEY PRICE, Aberdeen, 1959-61, *Belief*, pp. 460-1.

IV
THE KNOWLEDGE OF GOD

... *Natural Theology, in the widest sense of that term, in other words,*
'The Knowledge of God, the Infinite, the All, the First and Only
Cause, the One and Sole Substance, the Sole Being, the Sole Reality,
and the Sole Existence ...'.

Two Compulsory Questions

Two questions must confront a Gifford lecturer who seeks to try to give effect to Lord Gifford's purpose in the serious spirit in which it was meant. The first is: What do we mean by the word 'God'? The second is: How, in the light that in the twentieth-century philosophy has cast on Reality, must we conceive and speak of Him?

RICHARD BURDON HALDANE, St Andrews, 1902-04, *The Pathway to Reality*, Vol. 1, p. 15.

42

God as Absolute Being

Personality, to our view, is an essentially ethical category. A Person is a conscious being, whose life, temporally viewed, seeks its completion through deeds, while this same life, eternally viewed, consciously attains its perfection by means of a present knowledge of the whole of its temporal strivings. Now from our point of view, God is a Person. Temporally viewed, his life is that of the entire realm of consciousness in so far as, in its temporal efforts towards perfection, this consciousness of the universe passes from instant to instant of the temporal order, from act to act, from experience to experience, from stage to stage. Eternally viewed, however, God's life is the infinite whole that includes this endless temporal process, and that consciously surveys it as one life, God's own life. God is thus a Person, because, for our view, he is self-conscious, and because the Self of which he is conscious is a Self whose eternal perfection is attained through the totality of these ethically significant temporal strivings, these processes of evolution, these linked activities of finite Selves. We have long since ceased, indeed, to suppose that this theory means to view God's perfection, or his self-consciousness, as the temporal result of any process of evolution, or as an event occurring at the end of time, or at the end of any one process, however extended, that occurs in time. The melody does not come into existence contemporaneously with its own last note. Nor does the symphony come into full existence only when its last chord sounds. On the contrary

69

the melody is the whole, whereof the notes are but abstracted fragments; the symphony is the totality, to which the last chord contributes no more than does the first bar. And precisely so it is, as we have seen, with the relation between the temporal and the eternal order. God in his totality as the Absolute Being is conscious, not *in* time, but *of* time, and of all that infinite time contains. In time there follow, in their sequence, the chords of his endless symphony. For him is this whole symphony of life at once.

JOSIAH ROYCE, Aberdeen, 1899-1900, *The World and the Individual*, Vol. 2, pp. 418-19.

43

God—the Unknowable Absolute?

If the result of our scientific progress were to reduce the idea of God to that of an unknowable Être Suprême, religion would have no special interest in this spectre of its former greatness. For all it does is to preserve the consciousness that the finite cannot be conceived as a *res completa*—a whole bounded and terminated in itself. But if all that can really be known, all that can be made into a real interest of life, is assigned to the finite, the idea that there is a 'beyond' to which we can attach no definite predicate, can scarcely be considered of any practical importance. The consciousness of *such* an infinite would even seem to be the gift of an unfriendly destiny; for, so far as we paid any regard to it, it would tend to make us despise our proper work and all the aims to which our life is necessarily confined. It would be like a glimpse of a world beyond his prison walls to a prisoner who could never escape, and whose only wise course would be to shut his eyes and make the best of his bondage.

EDWARD CAIRD, St Andrews, 1890-2, *The Evolution of Religion*, Vol. 1, pp. 312-13.

44

The God Who Makes Himself Known

It is quite certain that all the theological affirmations defended by Plato, Lord Herbert and Spinoza were suggested to them in the first place by reflection upon living religious experience and could not have been suggested in any other way. But all living religious experience has been understood by those who enjoyed it as a two-sided affair, that is, as active intercourse between God and man. It is doubtful whether any race of men has ever believed that man could discover anything about God if God were not at the same time actively seeking to make himself known. Not even the most elementary practices of divination could proceed, if it were not believed that the gods themselves took the initiative in the provision of certain signs, omens and oracles such as could be interpreted by those in possession of the necessary skill. Cicero begins his treatise *On Divination* by saying that he knows 'of no nation, however polished and educated, or however brutal and barbarous', which does not share this belief. At all events it is certain that Christians have always believed that such knowledge as they can have of God is the fruit of a divine initiative whereby God seeks to make himself known. The faith of which it has spoken has always been conceived as a response to the divine approach. It is the apprehension of a divine communication.

We speak of this apprehension in frankly symbolic language as a hearing, and of this communcation as a speaking. God speaks and we hear his word. But of course we do not suppose that he speaks with lips of flesh or that we hear with our fleshly ears. We believe indeed that the words of Christ were divinely spoken, and that he spoke with lips of flesh, yet we do not say that what is divine in them can be received by our fleshly ears. It is only by 'the ear of faith' that we hear what they have to say to us, jut as it is only to 'the eye of faith' that his recorded deeds carry their divine message.

JOHN BAILLIE, Edinburgh, 1961-2, *The Sense of the Presence of God*, pp. 124-5.

45

The Question Man Cannot Put Aside

The knowledge of the one and only God, the knowledge *that* He is and *who* He is, is the knowledge of *faith*. Faith knowledge in the sense used by Reformed teaching does not mean a knowledge which is based merely on feeling, which is peculiar to the individual and which therefore has no binding character for others. On the contrary, no more objective and strict form of knowledge can exist, and no type of knowledge can lay claim more definitely to universal validity than the knowledge of faith. It is certainly true that it differs completely from anything else which man calls knowledge, not only in its content, but in its mode of origin and form as well. But this difference consists precisely in the fact that it is bound, a fact which excludes all arbitrariness and chance. The very question 'Who is God?' is not one of those questions which man puts to himself and is able either to put or not to put to himself. On the contrary, on every occasion that he raises it in earnest, he is *compelled* to raise it, because without his ever coming to think of it of his own accord, this question *is put* to him in such a way that it must be faced and cannot be evaded. Also in answering it he will not be able to choose, but he will have to obey—to read off, spell out and decipher the answer which is laid down for him. Faith knowledge is knowledge through revelation. And that simply means that it is a type of knowledge which is unconditionally bound to its object. And it is only to this object —only to God—that human thought can be bound in this way, since God Himself has bound it to Himself.

KARL BARTH, Aberdeen, 1937-8, *The Knowledge of God and the Service of God*, pp. 25-6.

46

Thou

The expression attributed in Genesis to God, 'I have sworn by myself,' means, Philo says:

None of the things which serve as warrants can be a firm warrant concerning God; for God has not shown His nature to any of them; He has made it invisible to the whole race. Who would have power to affirm positively that the Ground of the Universe is bodiless or that He is body, that He is of a certain quality *or that He is without qualities*, in a word to make any statement about His essence or character or mode of relations or movement? God alone can make an affirmation about

Himself, seeing that He alone knows His own nature infallibly and exactly (I. 159).

By calling God ἄποιος ('without qualities') Philo does not mean that He is without positive character. He only means that no human expression which attributes a particular quality to God can be adequate to the Reality. Every such statement is in some degree a mis-statement. The same thing some thinkers of our own time have expressed by saying that the only true mode of speech in regard to God is in the second person, 'Thou';[1] God is the supreme 'Thou'; in addressing himself directly to God, man can come into contact with the Ground of the Universe and have a sense of the Reality which touches him; but the moment he makes a statement about God in the third person—even though it is that God is good—he is more or less disfiguring the truth. To say indeed that God may properly be addressed as 'Thou' is in a way to state that He is personal, since you cannot with any meaning address an impersonal thing as 'Thou'; you give it a fictitious personality, if you do. Nevertheless, the thinkers we referred to would no doubt say that though your action in addressing God as 'Thou' was wholly right, nevertheless, if in your justification of it you bring in such a term as 'personal', if you make a statement about God in which by the copula 'is' personality, or anything else is attached to Him as something other than Himself, as an idea which can be applied to Him, then your form of words can be no more than a futile attempt to express the inexpressible.

EDWYN BEVAN, Edinburgh, 1933-4, *Symbolism and Belief*, pp. 20-1.

47

The Very Life of God

Few things are more disheartening to the philosophical student of religion than the way in which the implications of the doctrine of the Incarnation are evaded in popular theology by dividing the functions of the Deity between the Father and the Son, conceived practically as

---

[1] A footnote indicates reference to Karl Heim and Gabriel Marcel.

two distinct personalities or centres of consciousness, the Father perpetuating the old monarchical ideal and the incarnation of the Son being limited to a single historical individual. Grosser still, however, is the materialism which has succeeded in transforming the profound doctrine of the Spirit, as the ultimate expression of the unity and communion of God and man, into the notion of another distinct Being, a third centre of consciousness mysteriously united with the other two. The accidents of language have combined with the ingrained materialism of our ordinary thinking to make the doctrine of the Trinity a supra-rational mystery concerning the inner constitution of a transcendent Godhead, instead of the profoundest, and therefore the most intelligible, attempt to express the indwelling of God in man.

For if this is the deepest insight into human life, must we not also recognize it as the open secret of the universe? That is the conclusion to which we have been led: no God, or Absolute, existing in solitary bliss and perfection, but a God who lives in the perpetual giving of himself, who shares the life of his finite creatures, bearing in and with them the whole burden of their finitude, their sinful wanderings and sorrows, and the suffering without which they cannot be made perfect. It is the fundamental structure of reality which we are seeking to determine. For that surely is the meaning of all discussion as to the being and nature of God. In this ultimate instance, therefore, we cannot expect to gain an insight into that structure by passing altogether from the process of the finite life, treating it simply as an illusion, and defining Reality, in contrast with it, as the perpetual undimmed enjoyment of a static perfection. . . . We must interpret the divine on the analogy of what we feel to be profoundest in our own experience. And if so, the omnipotence of God will mean neither the tawdry trappings of regal pomp nor the irresistible might of a physical force. The divine omnipotence consists in the all-compelling power of goodness and love to enlighten the grossest darkness and to melt the hardest heart. 'We needs must love the highest when we see it.' It is of the essence of the divine prerogative to seek no other means of triumph—as, indeed, a real triumph is possible on no other terms. And thus, for a metaphysic which has emancipated itself from physical categories, the ultimate conception of is not that of a pre-existent Creator but, as it is for religion, that of the eternal Redeemer of the world. This perpetual process is the very life of God, in which, besides the effort and the pain, He tastes, we must believe, the joy of victory won.

ANDREW SETH PRINGLE-PATTISON, Aberdeen, 1912-13, *The Idea of God*, pp. 409-12.

The Beauty of God

The first and naïve question whether God is to be imagined as beautiful would be turned aside as irrelevant by the more advanced religions, and is only answered simply and strongly in the affirmative by the most anthropomorphic, namely the Greek. The perception of the divine personality as the transcendent embodiment of human beauty was at once the crowning achievement and the limitation of Greek religion; and we are only beginning to realize what such imagination meant for the art of the world. But the attribute of beauty had not much value for the Jewish religious imagination—and we are not sure what the Psalmist exactly meant when he exclaimed 'Out of Zion hath God appeared in perfect beauty'. There is no prominence of the idea of beauty as a divine attribute in Egyptian religion, except in the worship of the material divine sun; not so far as I am aware in Moslemism, nor in Mesopotamian or Vedic polytheisms. The association of the idea of beauty with the religious sphere, encouraged by the strong anthropomorphism of the Hellenes and by their unique artistic faculty and enthusiasm, was a distinctive feature of Greek philosophy, and especially the Platonic and Neoplatonic, reappearing at a later period in the religious theory of the Cambridge Platonists.[1] When Plotinus uses the beauty of the flowers as a proof of God's providence operating in the world, when St Augustine asserts that God is beautiful, that is to say, is the spiritual soul of beauty in created things, because the visible heavens and earth are beautiful, they are in accord with the experience not uncommon at the present day that deep perception of beauty in the world is one vehicle of communion with the divine spirit.

LEWIS RICHARD FARNELL, St Andrews, 1924-5, *Attributes of God*, pp. 210-12.

[1] Cf. *Cambr. Platon.* (Campagnac, p. 174): 'God is also that unstained Beauty and supreme Good which our wills are perpetually catching after: and wheresoever we find true Beauty, Love and Goodness, we may say, Here or there is God.'

Supra-Rational Theism

Religion has nothing whatever to lose, and has very much to gain, by a frank recognition that the qualities it ascribes to God have to be understood as only symbols or ideograms of the Divine Nature. I do not myself believe that this conclusion conflicts in any way with the general mood of religion, however sharply it may conflict with the main trends of dogmatic theology. When the plain question is put, 'Which is the more fit object of worship, a God whose power and goodness are in principle beyond human comprehension, or a God whose power and goodness differ not in kind but only in degree from the power and goodness to be found in His creation?' I confess I find it difficult to understand how a religious mind could hesitate long about giving its preference to the former.

CHARLES ARTHUR CAMPBELL, St Andrews, 1953-5, *On Selfhood and Godhood*, p. 361.

Beyond the Symbol?

All our effort to think true thoughts about God is an effort to get rid of the symbolical character of our conceptions, to change them from symbols into precise apprehensions. And if there has been any progress in thought about God between the primitive level and that of a twentieth century philosopher, progress has consisted in freeing conceptions from symbolical imagery. No one today in a civilized country who believes in God at all could deny that the process has been in large part successful: no one could now hold a view of God anthropomorphic in the same way in which the primitive conception was anthropomorphic. A Theist today would hold that his conception of God was less symbolic than that of the primitive man who thought of God as literally a person in human form living in the sky. But an intelligent Theist would also hold that this process of superseding symbols by precise apprehensions can never be complete. Any conception of God which man can reach must always be, more or less, a symbol still. And yet we must always go on trying to make our conceptions less symbolic, more precisely correspondent with the Reality. Only we must beware, when we do so, of supposing that we have got the truth behind a symbol because we substitute for the symbol a philosophic formula; such a formula may be less true than the symbol.

EDWYN BEVAN, Edinburgh, 1933-4, *Symbolism and Belief*, pp. 262-3.

51

Poetry and Science

The Truth apprehended by the Subconscious Psyche finds its natural expression in Poetry; the Truth apprehended by the Intellect finds its natural expression in Science. Poetry and Science have . . . to use the same vocabulary, because Man has only one vocabulary, and this has therefore to serve all Man's purposes. . . .

In either mode of apprehending the Truth, however, there can be either a vision of some particular feature or aspect of the Truth or a vision of the whole of it. On the poetic level of the Subconscious Psyche, the comprehensible vision is Prophecy;[1] on the scientific level of the Intellect it is Metaphysics. If our foregoing analysis of the difference between Poetry and Science is correct, it will follow that Prophetic Vision's attempt to present a comprehensive view of poetic truth must, in the very nature of the two modes of apprehension, be more feasible than the attempt made by Metaphysics to present a comprehensive view of scientific truth. No doubt, even the most illuminating prophetic utterance will fall infinitely far short of expressing poetic truth in its plenitude; 'for My thoughts are not your thoughts, neither are your ways My ways', saith the Lord. 'For as the Heavens are higher than the Earth, so are My ways higher than your ways, and My thoughts than

[1] 'Prophecy' in the original and authentic sense in which the word means, not a forecast of the future, but the revelation of a mystery that is out of the Intellect's reach. The literal meaning of 'prophecy' is the 'utterance' of Truth from a hidden source from which Truth cannot be extracted by intellectual processes.

your thoughts.' Nevertheless, a prophetic utterance may be, as far as it goes, an expression of absolute poetic truth. And this will be an expression of unique value, standing by itself, and not subject to abrogation, addition, or subtraction when confronted with other expressions, perhaps differing from it in the degree of their illumination, that have been uttered in other times and places. By contrast, the attempt made by Metaphysics to present a comprehensive view of scientific truth can never and nowhere be more than an interim provisional report on the general progress of Science up to date.

ARNOLD TOYNBEE, Edinburgh, 1952-3, *An Historian's Approach to Religion*, pp. 121, 123.

52

The Ultimate Reality

To me it seems that by God we mean, and can only mean, that which is most real, the Ultimate Reality into which all else can be resolved, and which cannot itself be resolved into anything beyond; that in terms of which all else can be expressed, and which cannot be itself expressed in terms of anything outside itself.

But this definition, the only definition which is at all adequate, enables us at the very commencement to rule out a number of conceptions which have often passed current, but which have never been used without getting the people who used them into difficulties. For example, you cannot talk of God, regarded as the Ultimate Reality, as a First Cause. That proves to be a totally inadequate metaphor, because cause and effect is a relationship that obtains and can obtain and have meaning only within the object world of experience, in the forms of Time and Space. Your problem is in point of fact directed to the existence and significance of that very object world itself. It is, in Kantian language, a transcendental problem. For it cannot be assumed that the explanation of Ultimate Reality can be found within the field of the object world, the nature and foundation of that field being one of the very aspects of things which falls within Reality. You cannot, therefore, speak of God as a $\Delta\eta\mu\iota\upsilon\rho\gamma\acute{o}\varsigma$, as a Creator of the Universe from the outside. He cannot stand to the world in the relation of a

Cause. For He must be independent of Space and Time, and we can attach no meaning to a Cause excepting as operative within Space and Time. We must reject that conception as wholly inadequate. Nor do we fare any better if we define God as a Substance. A substance is that which we know only in distinction from its attributes or its properties. The substance of that table is what I mean when I have abstracted from it in my mind all the properties by which I recognize it. Substance is a conception arrived at by negation, and has meaning in relation only to accidents or properties. To define God as Substance would, therefore, be to define Him as something relative, and not in the deepest sense of the word real. We must go further down for our foundations. Now there is one conception which, provisionally at least, we may use, because it is the one that does go deeper than any of these—the conception of God not as Substance but as Subject.

. . . Supposing that we could trace our globe back to a condition in which there was no life in it, at which it had only begun to assume shape as the gaseous matter had begun to solidify. What then? We should have eliminated life from the face of that globe; but still that globe, that solar system, that universe, that mass of gaseous and incandescent matter, would be there only as object for the subject. . . . Its time-duration would only have meaning to somebody who could conceive and measure it, so that past and present might be brought together and contrasted with the possible future. . . .

. . . And thus it comes about that even from the very beginning of things you have to presuppose mind, if you would speak in any language which is intelligible or communicable, and the deepest relation of all is that which you find when you go even to the very commencement of the Universe, the relation of being object for the subject.

RICHARD BURDON HALDANE, St Andrews, 1902-04, *The Pathway to Reality*, Vol. 1, pp. 19-23.

53

Some Aphorisms on the Nature of God

God is not to be treated as an exception to all metaphysical principles, invoked to save their collapse. He is their chief exemplification.

Viewed as primordial, he is the unlimited conceptual realization of the absolute wealth of potentiality. In this aspect, he is not *before* all creation, but *with* all creation.

But God, as well as being primordial, is also consequent. He is the beginning and the end. . . . He shares with every new creation its actual world.

The image—and it is but an image—the image under which this operative growth of God's nature is best conceived, is that of a tender care that nothing be lost.

The consequent nature of God is his judgment on the world. He saves the world as it passes into the immediacy of his own life. It is the judgment of a tenderness which loses nothing that can be saved. It is also the judgment of a wisdom which uses what in the temporal world is mere wreckage.

He does not create the world, He saves it: or, more accurately, He is the poet of the world, with tender patience leading it by his vision of truth, beauty and goodness.

ALFRED NORTH WHITEHEAD, Edinburgh, 1927-8, *Process and Reality*, pp. 486, 488, 490.

V

TRUE AND FELT KNOWLEDGE

I having been for many years deeply and firmly convinced that the true knowledge of God . . . the true and felt knowledge (not mere nominal knowledge) of the relations of man and the universe to Him . . . is the means of man's highest well-being and the security of his upward progress, I have resolved to institute . . . lectureships or classes for the teaching and diffusion of sound views regarding them, among the whole population of Scotland.

F

Theology is not Religion

Theology is not religion, but neither is ethical science morality, nor
aesthetical science the sense and enjoyment of beauty, nor grammar and
rhetoric the gift of speech. The sciences of Optics and Acoustics are
not meaningless because we can see and hear without a knowledge of
them, nor the sciences of Anatomy and Physiology, because the
knowledge of them is not necessary for the performance of bodily
functions. . . . In like manner, religion exists and must exist as a life
and experience before it can be made the object of reflective thought;
but there is no more reason, in this than in other instances, why
experimental knowledge should exclude scientific knowledge.

JOHN CAIRD, Glasgow, 1892-3 and 1895-6, *The Fundamental Ideas
of Christianity*, Vol. I, pp. 41-2.

What is Faith?

What, then, is faith? It is clearly impossible to identify faith with the
mere presence of an idea in the mind, or even with a belief in the truth
of that idea. It is not the former, for I may have an idea before my
mind without regarding it as corresponding to reality. Some thinkers,
for example, deny that the existence of an omniscient and omnipresent
God is capable of demonstration; but the very fact that the existence of
such a Being is denied, is sufficient evidence that it exists as an idea in
the mind of those who make the denial. To have the idea of an infinite
Being is therefore not the same thing as to have faith in the reality of
that Being. But, further, we may believe in the reality of God without
having, in the religious sense, faith in him. For, faith, in this sense of
the term, while it presupposes belief in its object, also involves an act
of will. I cannot have faith in God without having the conviction that
he is not a mere fiction of my own creation; but unless this conviction
is of such a character as to influence my life, it cannot be called faith,
in the religious sense of the word. Thus 'faith' is the expression of my
deepest and truest self; it is the spirit which determines the whole

character of my self-conscious life. To suppose that genuine faith should exist without being translated into action is therefore a contradiction in terms. The faith which has no influence on the life is not faith. Bearing this in mind we can understand why it has been maintained that religion has nothing to do with creeds and confessions. One may be perfectly familiar with a definite system of doctrine, and yet be entirely destitute of religious faith.

JOHN WATSON, Glasgow, 1910-12, *The Interpretation of Religious Experience*, Vol. 2, pp. 8-9.

56

Faith More than Probability

Faith contradicts nothing that science is in a position to affirm, and asserts nothing that science is in a position to deny. Science cannot disclaim it as error, nor can it appeal to science as truth. But what science can neither positively affirm nor positively deny may still count for something as being more or less probable; and 'probabilities are the guide of life'. In this sense the theist has been said to walk by faith and not by sight: he is not sure, it is said, but he hopes for the best and acts accordingly. Religious apologists sometimes argue on these lines— Pascal, Butler and Paley, for example—but the prudence thus advocated is not faith; and assuredly it is not religion. Its effect on the individual's conduct, if he gets no further, will be proportional to his estimate of the probability of what still remains uncertain.

JAMES WARD, St Andrews, 1907-10, *The Realm of Ends*, pp. 417-18.

57

Faith and Hypothesis

No man will commit his life to the care and guidance of a hypothesis recognized as such. What guides conduct must be assumed to be *ontologically* true, it must be a *faith*. But, for the scientific man to convert his hypothesis into a faith were to betray the very spirit of science.

A hypothesis must not turn into a dogma, and the scientific man is the servitor of no *creed*. Hypotheses, consequently, cannot transform character. They have no practical *vim*. They have by no means proven themselves, as religious faith has done, to be of all forces the strongest in man's history. The difference is vital and must not be obscured. . . . The sciences may conjecture, religion must '*know*': that is to say, it must be a matter experienced.

HENRY JONES, Glasgow, 1920-1, *A Faith that Enquires*, p. 83.

58

Faith and Reason

The only condition on which reason could have nothing to do with religion, is that religion should have nothing to do with truth. For in every controversy concerning what is or what is not truth, reason and not authority is the supreme arbiter; the authority that decides against reason commits itself to a conflict which is certain to issue in its defeat. The men who defend faith must think as well as the men who oppose it; their argumentative processes must be rational and their conclusions supported by rational proofs. If it were illicit for reason to touch the mysteries of religion, the Church would never have had a creed or have believed a doctrine, nor would man have possessed a faith higher than the mythical fancies which pleased his childhood. Without the exercise of reason we should never have had the Fourth Gospel or the Pauline Epistles, or any one of those treatises on the Godhead, the Incarnation, or the Atonement, from Athanasius to Hegel, or from Augustine to our own day, which have done more than all the decrees of all the Councils, or all the Creeds of all the Churches, to keep faith living and religion a reality. The man who despises or distrusts the reason despises the God who gave it, and the most efficient of all the servants He has bidden work within and upon man in behalf of truth. Here, at least, it may be honestly said there is no desire to build Faith upon the negation of Reason; where both are sons of God it were sin to seek to make the one legitimate at the expense of the other's legitimacy.

ANDREW MARTIN FAIRBAIRN, Aberdeen, 1891-3, *The Philosophy of the Christian Religion*, pp. 18-19.

From Subjectivism to Objectivity

We and God have business with each other; and in opening ourselves to his influence our deepest destiny is fulfilled. The universe, at those parts of it which our personal being constitutes, takes a turn genuinely for the worse or for the better in proportion as each one of us fulfills or evades God's demands. . . . Most religious men believe (or 'know', if they be mystical) that not only they themselves, but the whole universe of beings to whom God is present, are secure in his parental hands. There is a sense, a dimension, they are sure, in which we are *all* saved, in spite of the gates of hell and all adverse terrestrial appearances. God's existence is the guarantee of an ideal order that shall be permanently preserved. This world may indeed, as science assures us, some day burn up or freeze; but if it is part of his order, the old ideals are sure to be brought elsewhere to fruition, so that where God is, tragedy is only provisional and partial, and shipwreck and dissolution are not the absolutely final things. Only when this farther step of faith concerning God is taken, and remote objective consequences are predicted, does religion, as it seems to me, get wholly free from the first immediate subjective experience, and bring a *real hypothesis* into play. A good hypothesis in science must have other properties than those of the phenomenon it is immediately invoked to explain, otherwise it is not prolific enough. God, meaning only what enters into the religious man's experience of union, falls short of being an hypothesis of this more useful order. He needs to enter into wider cosmic relations in order to justify the subject's absolute confidence and peace.

WILLIAM JAMES, Edinburgh, 1901-02, *The varieties of Religious Experience*, pp. 507-8 (1952 edn).

Faith Transcends Knowledge

Faith is an extension beyond knowledge. From knowledge faith learns where and how to look, the unknown—the not impossible—takes its cue from the actually known.

Faith, therefore, is not blind. It does not ignore theoretical evidence; it does not fly in the face of facts or turn its back on them. There can be no justification for a belief which is contrary to the evidence. Faith is a belief which agrees with the evidence as far as it goes, but goes further. It lacks proof, but it may nevertheless be true and certain; for . . . neither truth nor certainty depend on proof.

Faith is not justified by the failure of knowledge, but by its only partial success. There is no hopefulness to be extracted from a general discrediting of science, but only by extending its credit. Faith does, nevertheless, profit by the limits of science.

RALPH BARTON PERRY, Glasgow, 1946-8, *Realms of Value*, p. 490.

61

The Essentially Religious Attitude

The religious consciousness has no special or exclusive connection with the supernatural, the other world or even the divine. It is essentially the attitude in which the finite being stands to whatever he at once fears and approves, in a word, to what he worships. It is impossible to draw the line at any point between the simplest experiences of this kind and those completest forms of devotion to which the term religion has been exclusively applied. Whatever makes us seem to ourselves worthless in our mere private selves, although or because attaching ourselves in the spirit to a reality of transcendent value, cannot be distinguished from religion.

Whenever then, we find a devotion which makes the finite self seem as nothing, and some reality to which it attaches itself seem as all, we have the essentially religious attitude.

The conclusion is, in a word, that the God of religion, inherent in the completest experience, is an appearance of reality, as distinct from being the whole and ultimate reality; a rank which religion cannot consistently claim for the supreme being as it must conceive him. But this conception, which finds him in the greater self recognized by us as present within the finite spirit, and as one with it in love and will, assigns him a higher reality, than any view which stakes everything on finding him to exist as a separate being after the model of a man. Religion establishes the infinite spirit because it is continuous with and present in the finite—in love and in the will for perfection. It does not need to appeal to facts of separate being, or to endeavour to demonstrate them. It is an experience of God, not a proof of him.

BERNARD BOSANQUET, Edinburgh, 1911-12, *The Value and Destiny of the Individual*, pp. 235, 255-6.

62

Religious Imagination

Imagination furnishes the means through which faith solves the problems that reason alone is unable to solve. God is a God of faith, not of thought; He appears in the kingdom of imagination, not in the system of categories; He appears on Mount Sinai; in the burning bush, in the still small voice, not in the absolute idea. The knowledge of God is a knowledge immanent in faith; it cannot be isolated and made logical and conceptual; it is an imaginative knowledge inherent not in the methodological and argumentative course of philosophical reasoning but rather in the unmethodical and naïve language of stories, tales, legends, proverbs, commandments, sermons, epistles, and so forth. Why is this so? Does the primitive and immature state of human culture require it? Should this prove true, we could at once go a step further and conclude that religion is altogether the product of such a primitive mentality, and that it must be replaced by empirical or metaphysical knowledge when the intellect has grown mature enough to recognize the truth without imaginative veils and figurative language. This conclusion needs only to be stated to be met with rejection.

Imagination owes its power to its peculiar nature. It is not, like sensation or intellect, confined to either the realm of sense reality or of intellectual notions and general concepts, but it belongs rather to both realms and it is therefore, suited to span the gulf between them. Imagination is at home in the sphere of change as well as in the sphere of changeless ideas; it is rooted as much in the visible as in the invisible

88

world: indeed, its peculiar excellency consists exactly in its capacity of making visible what is invisible and of detecting the invisible element in the visible situation. *Imagination binds together what the thinking mind separates;* or more precisely: it *maintains the original unity* of the elements separated by abstract thought. Imagination is as realistic as it is idealistic; it is as sensuous as it is intellectual: it moves in a medium in which the extremes are still united and undissolved.

The content of our intrinsically personal life, of our heart and destiny, our guilt and our longing, our love and our fear, our hope and our despair—the content of our real self—cannot be perceived or comprehended by reason alone. Whatever is personal stirs our imagination; it is imaginative in itself. This is the reason why the poet alone can describe life and why all merely scientific descriptions, be they ever so accurate within their own range, cannot disclose the unity of the outward and the inward aspects of experience, of its course and its meaning, of its appearance and its mystery. Imagination alone can perform this miracle, just because it is miraculous as compared with the naked senses and the sober intellect. The innermost kernel of life, however, is the relation to the ultimate mystery of life: this relation is the subject of faith. Therefore faith is necessarily imaginative.

RICHARD KRONER, St Andrews, 1939-40, *The Primacy of Faith*, pp. 137-9.

63

Not in Reason Alone

The idea of God is rooted in that ground [Faith], not in reason alone. Reason, unsupported by mystical intuition and religious imagination, remains destitute of the idea of God; it can and it should ascend to the idea of the perfect being, the *ens realissimum*, the supreme Self, the absolute truth, the absolute good and the absolute beautiful, but all these ideas present in part ideals which man erects as signs of the direction to be followed by his striving and working, in part problems not to be solved. *Religion solves these problems*; and it solves them by means of imagination. Since the ultimate goal of man is hidden from

89

reason, and the route to this goal is barred by antimonies, imagination is the only legitimate and appropriate tool of this solution, as revelation is the only legitimate and appropriate 'method' by which this solution is brought about.

Religious imagination is operative not only in figurative speech and metaphorical expressions, in symbolic ideas and legends, in miraculous occurrences and mystical thought, in poetical comparisons and suggestive parables; *it is operative in the very idea of God*. God, as religion depicts Him, as personal, as the willing and acting figure of the Old and the New Testament, as the Creator of the world, as the Lawgiver, Judge and Lord of men, as the Ruler of nature and of history, as the power of Providence and as the Father of Jesus Christ, the Redeemer and Saviour of all mankind—the living God is no rational idea or the content of such an idea, He is rather to be apprehended in the imagination alone; the idea of God is not a true *concept*, it is a holy *image*.

RICHARD KRONER, St Andrews, 1939-40, *The Primacy of Faith*, pp. 141-2.

64

Truth is Truth the World Over

Philosophers are wont to interpret works of art as embodiments of the beautiful and to regard beauty as the distinctively aesthetic value. I do not gainsay this, but it does not take us far enough. Plato, himself a consummate artist, knew better when he measured the worth of the artist's product by the standard of reason and truth. His error lay in restricting that standard to apprehension of universals, to the conceptual truth of the scientist or the philosopher. Of course, the artist when thus tested cuts a very sorry figure. Yet, why should a poetic image prove less effective as an instrument of knowledge than a 'logical construction'? We say, of a symphony of Beethoven, for instance, that it enables us not only to feel, but in some mysterious sense to 'see into the life of things', deepening and enriching our vision of reality. This, I grant, is vague language; the vision defies conceptual formulation; but if we deny its objectivity, what is left of the aesthetic experience? So in personal intercourse with our fellows; we come to know a man's true nature better, not worse, through the very intensity of our sympathetic emotion. Religion asserts that the same is true of man's personal intercourse with God. There is here no mere metaphor; truth is truth the world over, whether it be revealed by science or by art or by love of God or man. How, and in what measure, truth is reached by these diverse lines of approach is just the problem that calls for solution by philosophy.

WILLIAM GEORGE DE BURGH, St Andrews, 1938, *From Morality to Religion*, pp. 303-4.

65

The True Prophet of God

The great religious teacher is one in whom religious emotion is not only strong but also pure; and who, to preserve its purity, is quick to test by the dry light of reason the knowledge which such emotion seems to give him. When in such a one moral earnestness is joined to spiritual enthusiasm we ought to recognize a true prophet of God.

ERNEST WILLIAM BARNES, Aberdeen, 1927-9, *Scientific Theory and Religion*, p. 635.

66

The Deeper Source of Religion

I believe that feeling is the deeper source of religion, and that philosophic and theological formulas are secondary products, like translations of a text into another tongue. But all such statements are misleading from their brevity. . . .

When I call theological formulas secondary products, I mean that in a world in which no religious feeling had ever existed, I doubt whether any philosophic theology could ever have been framed. I doubt if dispassionate intellectual contemplation of the universe apart from inner unhappiness and need of deliverance on the one hand and mystical emotion on the other, would ever have resulted in religious philosophies such as we now possess. Men would have begun with animistic explanations of natural fact, and criticized these away into scientific ones, as they actually have done. In the science they would have left a certain amount of 'psychical research', even as they now will probably have to re-admit a certain amount. But high-flying speculations like those of either dogmatic or idealistic theology, these they would have no motive to venture on, feeling no need of commerce with such deities. These speculations must, it seems to me, be classed as over-beliefs, buildings-out performed by the intellect into directions of which feeling originally supplied the hint.

But even if religious philosophy had to have its first hint supplied by feeling, may it not have dealt in a superior way with the matter which feeling suggested? Feeling is private and dumb, and unable to give an account of itself. It allows that its results are mysteries and enigmas, declines to justify them rationally, and on occasion is willing that they should even pass for paradoxical and absurd. Philosophy takes just the opposite attitude. Her aspiration is to reclaim from mystery and paradox whatever territory she touches. To find an escape from obscure and wayward personal persuasion to truth objectively valid for all thinking men has ever been the intellect's most cherished ideal. To redeem religion from unwholesome privacy, and to give public status and universal right of way to its deliverances, has been reason's task.

I believe that philosophy will always have opportunity to labour at this task. We are thinking beings, and we cannot exclude the intellect from participating in any of our functions. Even in soliloquizing with ourselves, we construe our feelings intellectually. Both our personal ideals and our religious and mystical experiences must be interpreted congruously with the kind of scenery which our thinking mind inhabits. The philosophic climate of our time inevitably forces its own clothing on us. Moreover we must exchange our feelings with one another, and in doing so we have to speak, and to use general and abstract verbal formulas. Conceptions and constructions are thus a necessary part of our religion; and as moderator amid the clash of hypotheses, and mediator among criticisms of one man's constructions by another, philosophy will always have much to do.

WILLIAM JAMES, Edinburgh, 1901-02, *The Varieties of Religious Experience*, pp. 422-3 (1952 edn).

67

Faith—Truth

What kind of a truth is it, then, which is revealed to faith? It is not truth in the sense of knowing something, but in the sense of a divine-human, personal encounter. God does not reveal this and that; He does not reveal a number of truths. He reveals Himself by communicating Himself. It is the secret of His person which He reveals, and the secret of His person is just this, that He is self-communicating will; that God is Love.

EMIL BRUNNER, St Andrews, 1947-8, *Christianity and Civilization,* Vol. I, p. 37.

68

Mysticism

Mysticism is a spiritual philosophy which demands the concurrent activity of thought, will, and feeling. It assumes from the outset that these three elements of our personality, which in real life are never sundered from each other, point towards the same goal, and if rightly used will conduct us thither. Further, it holds that only by the consecration of these three faculties in the service of the same quest can a man become effectively what he is potentially, a partaker of the Divine nature and a denizen of the spiritual world. There is no special organ for the reception of Divine or spiritual truth, which is simply the knowledge of the world as it really is. Some are better endowed with spiritual gifts than others, and are called to ascend greater heights; but the power which leads us up the pathway to reality and blessedness is, as Plotinus says, one which all possess, though few use it.

This power is emphatically not a mere susceptibility to passionate or rapturous emotion. Mysticism has indeed been defined as 'an extension of the mind to God by means of the longing of love'; and there is nothing to quarrel with this definition. But it is 'the *Spirit* in love' of Plotinus, the *amor intellectualis Dei* of Spinoza, which draws us upward. It is the whole personality, unified and harmonized under the leadership of what the Stoics called the ruling faculty, that enters the holy of holies.

WILLIAM RALPH INGE, St Andrews, 1917-18, *The Philosophy of Plotinus*, Vol. 1, p. 5.

69

Ecstasy and the Life of God

The notion of ecstasy implies that, while we do not predicate identity of any finite creaturely being with the mystical pole of the universe, neither do we ever predicate sheer otherness of them. We allow the possibility that a finite creaturely being can *become* one with the mystical pole of the universe, can be brought into coincidence with it, which coincidence does not, however, exclude the possibility of a subsequent falling apart. Each finite creaturely being has its ecstasy, its appropriate going beyond itself into the mystical pole of unity, where it also becomes one with everything else, and this ecstasy is no strange emotional exaltation but a necessary limiting possibility of creaturely being, and also, in a reverse regard, of eternal, non-creaturely being. In the case of inert matter, ecstasy seems merely a thinkable possibility, though the sacrament of the altar perhaps furnishes a valid counter-example: stock and stones, we may say, are too securely lodged on the periphery of being to retreat into their absolute source and re-emerge refurbished and shining. But conscious beings are capable of a transformation and reduction to that pure zeal for impersonal good which is also the core of their being, as of everything else, and, to the extent that this takes place, the distinction between conscious being and deity becomes altogether formal, like the distinction between an ellipse whose minor focus is zero and a straight line. In our 'highest moments' we feel ourselves to be mere extensions, expressions of an all-perfect absolute, and, since this absolute is not a person among persons external to finite persons as they are external to one another—though at certain stages in cosmic history it may well seem to be so—there is no reason to think that there is anything intrinsically false in such feelings. The ecstasies we have mentioned extend to the ordinary ecstasies of devoted, dedicated

94

persons of all sorts, though there are, of course, ecstasies of a more full-fledged trance-like type, involving loss of ordinary consciousness for a period.

JOHN NIEMAYER FINDLAY, St Andrews, 1964-6, *The Transcendence of the Cave*, p. 187.

VI

THE LIMITATIONS OF GOD?

The lecturers shall be under no restraint whatever in their treatment of their theme; for example, they may freely discuss (and it may be well to do so) . . . whether God is under any or what limitations, and so on, as I am persuaded that nothing but good can result from free discussion.

The Limitations of God

The idea of a God in some way limited is not necessarily repugnant to advanced religion, and we find Origen accepting it without scruple.[1] It certainly lends itself to dualism, for it implies some other force or substance or principle other than God which limits him. And this implication is in accord with the main current of Greek philosophy, which is dualistic in spite of Plato, and which so far as it deals seriously with the great religious problem of evil, is less concerned to champion the doctrine of 'monism' or the unlimited divine omnipotence as to purify the concept of God's character from any imputation of evil and to shield him from any responsibility for it. It inclines therefore to the view that God did not create matter and that though matter is not intrinsically evil there is some quality of stubborn resistance in matter that prevents it being shaped in accordance with the perfect divine idea and to the perfect form that God would impress upon it. An echo of this thought is in Matthew Arnold's phrase—'the something that infects the world'. This Greek view is fortified by the stimulating thought which finds some expression in Greek literature that the divine power and goodness are shown by the providential skill whereby evil can be turned into good at the last.

LEWIS RICHARD FARNELL, St Andrews, 1924-5, *The Attributes of God*, pp. 277-8.

The Creator God

The Biblical doctrine of the Creator, and the world as His creation, is itself not a doctrine of revelation, but it is basic for the doctrine of revelation. It expresses perfectly the basic Biblical idea of both the

[1] *Vide* Origen's fragment quoted by Rashdall, *The Idea of Atonement in Christian Theology*, p. 268.

transcendence of God and His intimate relation to the world. The doctrine is expressed in a 'mythical' or supra-rational idea. Genetically the idea of creation is related to primitive concepts in which God is pictured as fashioning the world as the potter moulds his clay. The Bible retains this 'primitive' concept because it preserves and protects the idea of the freedom of God and His transcendence. These are lost or imperilled by the more rational concept of 'first cause' (which takes the place of God in naturalistic philosophies), and by the concept of a form-giving *nous*, which creates by forming the previously formless stuff or matter (which is the basic conception of divinity in idealistic philosophies).

The doctrine of creation preserves the transcendence and freedom of God without implying that the created world is evil because it is not God. On the contrary Biblical religion consistently maintains the goodness of creation precisely on the ground that it is created by God. In this doctrine of the goodness of creation the foundation is laid for the Biblical emphasis upon the meaningfulness of human history. History is not regarded as evil or meaningless because it is involved in the flux of nature, and man is not regarded as evil because he is dependent upon a physical organism. The doctrine of creation escapes the error of the naturalists who, by regarding causality as the principle of meaning, can find no place for human freedom and are forced to reduce man to the level of nature. It escapes the errors of the rationalists who make *nous* into the ultimate principle of meaning, and are thereby tempted to divide man into an essentially good reason, which participates in or is identified with the divine, and an essentially evil physical life.

REINHOLD NIEBUHR, Edinburgh, 1939, *The Nature and Destiny of Man*, Vol. 1, pp. 143-4.

72

Human Freedom

If ethical theism is to stand, the evil in the world cannot be referred to God in the same way as the good is referred to him; and the only way to avoid this reference is by the postulate of human freedom. This freedom must be a real freedom, so that it may account for the actual choice of evil when good might have been chosen. We have therefore to face the inference that there is a limitation of the divine activity: that things occur in the universe which are not due to God's will, though they must have happened with his permission, that is, through his self-limitation. Nor does this view justify the objection that we are making the divine nature finite; for, if it is conceived as limited, it is not limited by anything outside itself. Rather we may say that a higher range of power and perfection is shown in the creation of free beings than in the creation of beings whose every thought and action are pre-determined by their Creator.

On the other hand, individual freedom is not, and cannot be, un-limited: otherwise each free being would require a world of his own, and there would be no universe. And clearly man's freedom is restricted by the conditions both of heredity and of environment. The range of his selection is limited by the experience which gives content to his life, as well as by the inherited tendencies which are his from the beginning of his career. These afford ample opportunity for freedom in the development of his activity, but not unrestricted openings for any and every kind of life. A man cannot at will choose to be a mathematician, an artist, a statesman, or even a millionaire. But there is one form of activity which is never closed, and that is the realization of moral values: one choice before every man, the choice of good or evil.

WILLIAM RITCHIE SORLEY, Aberdeen, 1914-15, *Moral Values and the Idea of God*, pp. 469-70.

73

Love Must Have an Object

The religious man, like Enoch, 'walks with God'. A light, like that of the Shekinah, always shines upon his path. He has no will of his own in an exclusive sense; and there is a sense in which not even his personality is any longer his own. These are familiar experiences. Are they possible if God dwells apart and contemplates for ever his own perfection? Would they be possible were God the monarchic Ruler, or the Stern Judge demanding a *quid pro quo* in the blood of a redeemer in return for forgiveness of sins? Or are not all these conceptions irreconcilable with the fundamental truth of the religion of love?

Philosophy has performed only a portion of its task in showing how the finite world implies the Absolute. It must also show what necessities, if any, dwell in the absolute, and account for its eternal outgoing and expression of itself in objects. It is not only true that 'the finite world cannot be conceived to be complete and independent, and that its existence must therefore be referred back to God', but also as Caird said, that 'in the nature of God there is a necessity and reason for the existence of the world'. To the question sometimes asked, 'Why did God come out of his isolated perfection so as to complete himself only through the medium of the Universe?' the answer is relatively simple. It is given in the conception of God as Love. Love *must* have an object. Philosophy gives an answer which, in the last resort, is the same. Absoluteness undoubtedly implies that self-completeness, that positive and commanding relation to objects, that possession of its own experience, which are involved in self-consciousness. A self-conscious being which has no object and does not possess its opposite, and affirm its unity in terms of it, is impossible. Hence an Absolute without a world is empty nothingness, just as a world without the Absolute is impossible. Nature is the experience, the living operation of the Absolute, and the Absolute is not only omnipresent in it, but real in virtue of it. It is as manifesting itself that the Absolute, on its part, lives and moves and has its being.

HENRY JONES, Glasgow, 1920-1, *A Faith that Enquires*, pp. 273-4.

74

Purpose and Promise

It is difficult to shut out the impression that Nature is Nature for a purpose. We do not think any longer of a 'directive power' outside of the evolving organisms, but of a directive power which is bone of their bone and flesh of their flesh—a directive power analogous to that which we ourselves know when we command our course or send an arrow to its mark. What we must particularly take account of is the main trend in evolution, making persistently for the dominance of mentality and the establishment eventually of personality. Whether what we now experience be the goal or near the goal, it gives significance to the whole long journey. And if Man be the highest product of evolution, and if the central reality in our life is our clear purpose, may we not ask whether there is not also a purpose at the core of the world-process?
. . . We must, however, recognize that just as Man's conceived purpose transcends the mammal's perceived purpose, as that in turn transcends the lower animal's ingrained or organized purposiveness, so, but much more, will the Divine Purpose transcend our highest thoughts of it.

But we deem that if we err in using the word Purpose—the biggest word we have—we err less grievously than if we used no word at all.

For millions and millions of years there was throughout Nature no voice of life at all—nothing to break the silence but the thunder and the cataract, the waves on the shore, and the wind among the trees. The morning stars sang together and the little hills clapped their hands, but there was no voice of life at all. The long lasting silence was first broken by insects, but they never got beyond instrumental music. It is to the progressive Amphibians of the Carboniferous Age that we must look back with special gratefulness, for they were the first to get vocal cords, and, interestingly enough, a movable tongue. With them Animate Nature found a voice.

In a much deeper sense, however, we may say that for millions and millions of years Nature was speechless—never more than groaning and whispering, as it were. It was in Man that Nature became definitely articulate; that the inherent rationality was echoed. In poem and painting Man expresses his aesthetic appreciation and partial understanding of the system of which he forms a part; in his science he turns darkness into light; in the application of science he conquers and controls the world.

JOHN ARTHUR THOMSON, St Andrews, 1915-16, *The System of Animate Nature*, Vol. 2, pp. 642-4.

75

The End in the Realm of Ends

We have been contemplating the universe as a realm of ends. If we were asked what is the end of this realm of ends we might answer rightly enough that its end can only be itself; for there is nothing beyond it, and no longer any meaning in beyond. It is the absolutely absolute. Still within it we have distinguished the One and the Many, and we have approached it from the standpoint of the latter. In so doing we are liable to a bias, so to say, in favour of the Many: led to the idea of God as ontologically and teleologically essential to their completion, we are apt to speak as if he were a means for them. Those who attempt to start from the standpoint of the One betray a bias towards the opposite extreme. The world, on their view, is for the glory of God: its ultimate *raison d'être* is to be the means to this divine end. Can we not transcend these one-sided extremes and find some sublimer idea which shall unify them both? We can indeed; and that idea is Love. But here again we trench on the mystical, the ineffable, and can only speak in parables. Turning to Christianity as exhibiting this truth in the purest form we know, we find it has one great secret—dying to live, and one great mystery—the incarnation. The love of God in creating the world implies both. *Leiblichkeit ist das Ende aller Wege Gottes*, said an old German theologian. The world is God's self-limitation, self-renunciation might we venture to say? And so God is love. And what must that world be that is worthy of such love? The only worthy object of love is just love: it must then be a world that can love God. But love is free: in a ready-made world then it could have no place. Only as we learn to know God do we learn to love him: hence the long and painful discipline of evolution, with *its* dying to live—the converse process to incarnation—the putting off the earthly for the likeness of God. In such a realm of ends we trust 'that God is love indeed, and love creation's final law'. We cannot live or move without faith, that is clear. Is it not then rational to believe in the best, we ask; and can there be a better?

JAMES WARD, St Andrews, 1907-10, *The Realm of Ends*, pp. 452-3.

76

Nature Indicted

J. S. Mill, in his essay on 'Nature', framed a terrible indictment against the callousness, cruelty, and injustice exhibited in the ordinary course of natural phenomena.

In sober truth (he writes) nearly all the things which men are hanged or imprisoned for doing to one another, are nature's every day performances. . . . Nature impales men, breaks them as if on the wheel, casts them to be devoured by wild beasts, burns them to death, crushes them with stones like the first Christian martyr, starves them by the quick or slow venom of her exhalations, and has hundreds of other hideous deaths in reserve, such as the ingenious cruelty of a Nabis or a Domitian never surpassed.

Mill drew the conclusion that the God who is responsible for Nature, as he describes it, cannot be a Being both of unlimited power and unlimited goodness. In a later essay, Mill maintained that all the evidence from design, and from the characteristics of Nature, point to a Deity whom he describes as:

A Being of great but limited power, how or by what limited we cannot even conjecture; of great, and perhaps unlimited intelligence but perhaps, also, more narrowly limited than his power; who desires, and pays some regard to, the happiness of his creatures, but who seems to have other motives of action which he cares more for, and who can hardly be supposed to have created the universe for that purpose alone. Such is the Deity whom Natural Religion points to; and any idea of God more captivating than this comes only from human wishes, or from the teaching of either real or imaginary Revelation.

The general picture of organic evolution painted by modern Biology is one in which the struggle for existence and nutriment, involving pain and death, is an important and possibly a dominant feature, although its repulsive aspect may perhaps sometimes have been drawn in too lurid colours. The ruthless sacrifice of multitudes of individuals appears to be a feature of the ordinary course of evolution; it has been said that Nature cares nothing for the individual, but much for the race. The facts brought to light by Bacteriology and Parasitology have disclosed the existence of many organisms, and of what have the appearance of being most ingenious contrivances, the apparent purpose of which is to inflict torture and death upon other, and usually higher organisms. . . . A consistent theist must regard as, in some sense, God's creatures, those living organisms whose presence and activities condition the existence of tetanus, cholera, typhus, and many other diseases. The contemplation of this aspect of phenomena gives rise to a very real problem, not only for Theologians, but for great numbers of thoughtful persons.

ERNEST WILLIAM HOBSON, Aberdeen, 1921-22, *The Domain of Natural Science*, pp. 497-8.

77

Physical Pain

The problem of physical pain is (especially to some imaginations—not generally those of the sufferers themselves) a burden which they cannot bear. I need not attempt to repaint the picture of the waste and torture evident in the process of nature as it has been so often and so vividly portrayed. But I must briefly enumerate the reductions and qualifications which need to be made on such estimates.

(1) We must recognize the even gross element of exaggeration in some of these pictures, particularly as regards the pain of animals, outside the area of human cruelty and carelessness. The abundant happiness of animal life is ignored. (2) We must recognize how vast a proportion of the whole amount of recognizable suffering in the world has been due directly or indirectly to human selfishness, pride and lust. (3) We must acknowledge that the world is a system of coherent parts, and that the alleged cruelties of the system may be, and indeed appear to be, inevitable conditions, at least in great part, of any world system and gradual development; whereas if there were no 'cosmos', existence would be unendurable. (4) We must own the vast difference made to the problem, so far as pain affects man himself, when our eyes are opened to the truth embodied in the Cross of Christ, that all that is most noble and that approaches perfection in humanity is seen in obvious experience to be the fruit of sacrifice—of pain willingly endured; while for the disastrous effects of pain unwillingly endured we must hold the rebel will responsible. (5) We must recognize that Christ was very far from acquiescing in the suffering and the disease which He saw around Him. He saw in it, at least in great part, a monstrous invasion of the world of God by a hostile power. 'An enemy hath done this'; 'Satan hath bound this woman'... He certainly meant His Church to be a fellowship of men bent on 'Rebellion' against the world of needless suffering. (6) We must remember that the picture of suffering in this world is altogether altered in its perspective for one who believes that this world is only the vestibule of the true life, the place for soul-making and kingdom-building.

CHARLES GORE, St Andrews, 1929-30, *The Philosophy of the Good Life*, pp. 334-6.

78

Living with Suffering

If the doctor's account of my illness as a breakdown in an apparatus is inadequate, the priest who comes to visit me and tells me to regard the illness as a trial or tribulation inflicted on me by God is not in much better case; for he also places himself outside the troublesome and mysterious reality which is that of my illness itself. Just like the man for whom I am merely a machine, the priest shows himself incapable of transcending the plane of causality. But it is just that transcendence which is necessary here, and it is only on condition that we effect such a transcendence that we can acknowledge the mystery of our illness. But let me express myself more strictly: to recognize my illness as a mystery, is to apprehend it as being a presence, or as being a modification of a presence. What we are essentially concerned with is somebody other than ourselves in so far as he is a sick man, or it would be better to say with my neighbour and the call he is making on me—the call to show myself compassionate and helpful. In the case, however, where it is I myself who am ill, my illness becomes a presence to me in the sense that I have to live with it, as with some room-mate whom I must learn to get along with as best I can; or again the illness becomes a presence in so far as those who care for me, and play the part of a Thou to me in my need, become intermediaries between me and it. Of course, in the case in which my illness has utterly prostrated me, in a state either of complete collapse or acute pain, my illness, paradoxically, ceases, as a separate presence, to exist for me; I no longer keep up with it that strange acquaintanceship which can be a struggle, or a dangerous flirtation, or the oddest blend of both.

One might develop these remarks at length in order to show how suspicious we ought to be of those lectures on illness which people seem so specially apt to deliver if they have never been seriously ill themselves: what rude health they always seem to enjoy, those bluff haranguers of the sick! Quite literally, they do not know what they are talking about, and their smug loquacity has something very insolent about it when we consider the terrible reality they are faced with, a reality which they ought at least to respect.

GABRIEL MARCEL, Aberdeen, 1949-50, *The Mystery of Being*, Vol. I, pp. 209-10.

79

Innocent Suffering

Children are born into the world crippled in body or diseased in mind through no fault of their own, and are not even allowed to perish. Millions, who escape the worst conditions, yet grow up with organizations or under conditions that make the true life of a human being impossible for them—men and women whose intellectual and moral failure cannot, in common justice, be counted to them for sin. We have children's hospitals full of cripples and semi-imbeciles. An unheeding and inexorable nature seems to pursue its way relentlessly, here lifting up and there casting down. What Hume says of the animal world is much more conspicuous and appalling in the man-world. . . .

'Suffering,' says Huxley, 'is an essential constituent of the cosmic process.' Humanity bears a cross. In what we see, a 'further' is involved, if the End be The Good. And when we contemplate the frequent superfluity and cruel purposelessness of evil, the contemplation forces on us the further conviction that the Divine life has, at this stage of its unfolding, to encounter difficulties which it cannot wholly overcome, but which the actual good we see and the ideals of reason force us to believe mediate a higher and better. We men are sharing the pain of God Himself: we are partners in His cosmic difficulty. Our personal hope is in death, our victory is the grave. This world is a promise; our life an infancy; our knowledge in the last resort a prescience.

Let us have faith that the absolute idea—the initiating all-comprehending Thought—contains the issues of the finite. The finite is as negation *within* the Absolute Synthesis; it is the method of procedure whereby God lives, and can alone live, as a revelation in Space and Time. There is a necessity in the method; but it is a necessity from within, not a coaction from without. The finite, vast as it is, is not so vast as the Infinite Being in whom all is One. The finite is within Him, and all is being worked out by Him into a conciliated Harmony when God shall be all in all.

SIMON SOMERVILLE LAURIE, Edinburgh, 1905-06, *Synthetica*, Vol. 2, pp. 325-6, 339.

80

God's Hatred of Evil

The complete good includes evil only as something to be hated and abolished. The Universal Mind must therefore hate it in a degree which to us is incomprehensively great. How are we to represent this to ourselves from our finite point of view? We can do so only in terms of our own experience. But we learn to hate evil, as we ought to hate it, in suffering from it, and by the struggle against it in ourselves and in others. Are we then to think of the Eternal Mind as suffering in this way? Are we to ascribe to it sentiments and emotions such as we feel ourselves? Clearly the truth must be widely removed from this. The Eternal Mind is above the ebb and flow of things; it is 'rest at the heart of endless agitation'.

Yet if we try to escape altogether this sort of anthropomorphism we inevitably fall into another which is incomparably more false and mischievous. We tend to think of the Eternal Mind as enjoying an Epicurean calm, aloof from the struggle and evil in which finite individuals are immersed. We regard it as a spectator of the battlefield, but not as itself involved in the strife. But this way of correcting anthropomorphism takes a fundamentally false direction. It is just as if we were to represent the divine knowledge as ignorance, merely because all analogies drawn from knowledge in finite things are essentially inadequate to convey positive insight into the nature of an Infinite and Eternal Being as such. Divine knowledge differs from ours in being more than we can understand, not in being less than we can understand. Similarly when we say that God hates evil, the word 'hate' is misleading in so far as we are unable in imagination to divest hatred of the forms which it assumes in finite beings. But let us make no mistake about the nature and direction of the error. We err not because the Divine antagonism to evil is less than we can figure to ourselves through finite analogies, but because it is incomprehensively greater. 'The Lord God is a consuming fire' and 'Man of War'. He is so because He is Love, and His tender mercies are over all His works.

The same holds good for suffering in finite beings. This must, I venture to think, have its incomprehensible counterpart in the Divine nature. This may appear a hazardous position. But I cannot think that it is too bold, when I consider the appeal made to the religious consciousness by the Christian doctrine of a crucified God. It is significant also that the Christian creed corrects what might otherwise be too anthropomorphic in its teaching by holding that it is God the Son and not God the Father who suffers. In one respect of His nature He is truly represented as participating in the misery of finite being. In another He is eternally triumphant and enjoys eternal blessedness.

GEORGE FREDERICK STOUT, Edinburgh, 1919-21, *God and Nature*, pp. 323-5.

81

Progress by Sacrifice

If God's relation to human experience be one of immanence, then He is much more than a spectator of the self-sacrifice by which progress is promoted: He is in it, a fellow-sufferer. Still more clearly is this true if in Christ God be incarnate. That conception may labour under metaphysical difficulties, but on the ethical side it is worthy of all acceptation. It makes God a moral hero, a burden-bearer for His own children, a sharer in the sorrow and pain that come on the good through the moral evil that is in the world.

ALEXANDER BALMAIN BRUCE, Glasgow, 1897-8, *The Providential Order*, p. 369.

82

God the Fellow-sufferer

There are four creative phases in which the universe accomplishes its actuality. There is first the phase of conceptual origination, deficient in actuality, but infinite in its adjustment of valuation. Secondly, there is the temporal phase of physical origination, with its multiplicity of actualities. In this phase full actuality is attained; but there is deficiency in the solidarity of individuals with each other. This phase derives its determinate conditions from the first phase. Thirdly, there is the phase of perfected actuality, in which the many are one everlastingly, without the qualification of any loss either of individual identity or of completeness of unity. In everlastingness, immediacy is reconciled with objective immortality. This phase derives the conditions of its being from the two antecedent phases. In the fourth phase, the creative action completes itself. For the perfected actuality passes back into the temporal world, and qualifies this world so that each temporal actuality includes it as an immediate fact of relevant experience. For the kingdom of heaven is with us today. The action of the fourth phase is the love of God for the world. It is the particular providence for particular occasions. What is done in the world is transformed into a reality in heaven, and the reality in heaven passes back into the world. By reason of this reciprocal relation, the love in the world passes into the love in heaven, and floods back again into the world. In this sense, God is the great companion—the fellow-sufferer who understands.

ALFRED NORTH WHITEHEAD, Edinburgh, 1927-8, *Process and Reality*, pp. 496-7.

VII

PROMOTING AND ADVANCING
THE TRUE KNOWLEDGE OF GOD

And my desire and hope is that these lectureships and lectures may promote and advance among all classes of the community the true knowledge of Him Who is, and there is none and nothing besides Him, in Whom we live and move and have our being.

St Paul, Apologist and Natural Theologian

In his speech at Athens (delivered before an audience of Athenians, who crowded to hear an address from one whom they understood to be a candidate for recognition in the leading university of the world) he quotes from 'your own poets' half a line of Aratus, and also a line, 'in Him we live and move and exist', whose metrical character is disguised by transformation from the Ionic dialect to the Attic and from the second person to the third. The changes, needed to suit the address, show the Apostle's usual freedom. His words imply that he made at Athens quotations from different poets, although the plain meaning was disregarded by modern commentators, until Professor (Rendel) Harris saw the truth:

He is not far from each one of us, for 'in Him we live and move, and have our being', as certain of your poets have said, 'for we also are his offspring'.

The orator, addressing an educated audience, presses into his service quotations from philosophic poetry which was familiar to society at that time and harmonious with its spirit. . . .[1]

The Blessed Paul, surveying the religious monuments and institutions of the great centre of learning for the Greek world, was struck with the altar 'to an unknown god', which rightly or wrongly he regarded as one of those raised in accordance with the instructions of Epimenides, and the connexion recalled to his mind a familiar passage of the Cretan poet, which he quoted in part to Titus. When he was required to address the Court of Areopagus, he took as his text the inscription on this altar and the lines in which Epimenides expressed his conviction about the Eternal God and His relation to man. This 'unknown god' of the altar was at once a witness to the religious feeling hidden deep in the minds of the Athenians and a confession of ignorance of His true nature. Their own poets had taught truth regarding Him; but it remained for the modern teaching to reveal it fully.

WILLIAM MITCHELL RAMSAY, Edinburgh, 1915-16, *Asianic Elements in Greek Civilization*, pp. 33-5.

[1] There follows here the evidence for Epimenides' authorship of the line 'in him we live and move and exist'. The quotation from Titus I. 12. comes from the same poem, though Ramsay does not necessarily endorse the Pauline authorship of the epistle.

84

The Modern Predicament

The work of intellectual reformation is bound to be a thankless one.
It may have to lay its hands on the dearest idols of the past—to break
with much that is embedded, not only in the language of theology, but
in the traditional language of religion itself. Criticism is not a religious
exercise, even though it may be carried on in a religious spirit; and it
may seem to empty religion and so to weaken its appeal. Yet religion,
which has always to struggle against spurious sentiment and twisted
morality, must today free itself also from the primitive science and false
history it has taken over from an earlier age. In the ancient and medieval
worlds, where there was no vast gulf between the religious and the
secular views, it was easier to adjust them to one another than it is under
present conditions. Good men who reject theological dogmatism may
still attach themselves to religious institutions in which they find the
elements of grace; but until theology can be adapted to its modern
scientific background and so can recover its ancient integrity, not only
will the indifferent masses remain indifferent, but many men and women
who either are, or long to be, religious in heart will continue to live
their lives outside the Churches, especially if these treat honest attempts
at criticism—not to mention one another—with hostility or intolerance....

A revival of religion will never come by mere thinking, not even by
religious thinking; but without a supreme effort of thought which will
satisfy the mind as well as the heart, religion will not easily recover its
former influence or restore to men the spiritual wholeness which many
of them prize but seek in vain.

HERBERT JAMES PATON, St Andrews, 1949-50, *The Modern
Predicament*, pp. 386-7.

85

Call to Pilgrimage

You cannot anywhere, whether in life or in logic, find rest and salvation
by withdrawing from the intercourse and implications of life; no more
in the world of individual property and self-maintenance than in the

world of international politics and economics; no more in the world of logical apprehension than in that of moral service and religious devotion. Everywhere to possess reality is an arduous task; stability and solidity are not in the beginning, but if anywhere, only in proportion as we enter upon the larger vistas of things. . . .

Starting with this attitude and perception, we see that if our Pilgrim's Progress is adventurous, it is beyond a doubt inevitable. To cling to our initial standing ground—or to strive or pretend to do so, for it is not really possible—is without any question to abide in the City of Destruction. The idea of a solid given—a personality, a fact, an apprehension, which we possess *ab initio*, and are tempted rashly and perversely to abandon in the quest of the Absolute, is an illusion which has no warrant in vital experience. The road of philosophical speculation is not the possible way for most men, nor the only way for any man; that is true and sound. But in one way and another, in labour, in learning, and in religion, every man has his pilgrimage to make, his self to remould and acquire, his world and his surroundings to transform. . . . And it is in this adventure, and not apart from it, that we find and maintain the personality which we suppose ourselves to possess *ab initio*.

BERNARD BOSANQUET, Edinburgh, 1911-12, *The Principle of Individuality and Value*, pp. 7-9.

86

The Only Method

Reliance on authority instead of reason is often passed off as a modest deference to skilled opinion; in fact, it is pure scepticism.

An unhesitating appeal to reason as our only test of truth seems to be not only an admissible method of study, but the only method of study consistent with regard to truth, and the only method which can issue in serious beliefs.

HENRY MELVILL GWATKIN, Edinburgh, 1904-05, *The Knowledge of God*, Vol. 1, p. 3.

Authority

Now it is universally recognized that religious belief, like all other, rests at first on authority.[1] There is here no relevant difference between a child brought up by religious parents and a full-grown unbeliever converted by the appeal of the preacher. In the latter case the act of surrender is more conscious, and it is also more conspicuous because surrender is a less frequent occurrence in the life of an adult than in that of a child. But it is still, in both cases, surrender. The number of instances in which a man becomes in a living sense religious by argumentation must be extremely small.

The child accepts what he is told concerning God as he accepts all else that he is told by those in trust upon whom he lives, according to his capacity to receive it. In the same way he accepts the dogmatic assertion that $7 \times 7 = 49$ without working it out for himself. But in most departments of life the basis of belief is gradually shifted from the authority of parents and teachers to his own experience and his own reflection upon this. And so far as this happens, his belief becomes more autonomous. It is his own; he has verified and vindicated it. He is still grateful to parents and teachers—more grateful now than ever. But his belief no longer rests on their authority. He has put it to the proof himself; very likely in so doing he has modified it; but in any case it is now his own, not something which he has borrowed from others.

WILLIAM TEMPLE, Glasgow, 1932-4, *Nature, Man and God*, pp. 19-20.

[1] It is important to remember that there is no contrast between Reason and Authority. It is impossible to accept a belief on Authority except so far as the Authority is accepted by Reason. In so far as a child's acceptance of what he is told is *totally* uncritical, that is not acceptance on Authority, but on the causal-action of impressions received. His belief rests on Authority only when his acceptance of what he is told is due to trust in those who tell.

The Theistic Arguments

The arguments for God's existence have stood for hundreds of years with the waves of unbelieving criticism breaking against them, never totally discrediting them in the ears of the faithful, but on the whole slowly and surely washing out the mortar from between their joints. If you have a God already whom you believe in, these arguments confirm you. If you are atheistic, they fail to set you right.

WILLIAM JAMES, Edinburgh, 1901-02, *The Varieties of Religious Experience*, pp. 427-8.

Three Arguments for the Truth of Religion

1. There is, in the first place, a strong presumption from analogy that the principles of religion are valid, and that the outcome of the historical process has been good and trustworthy. To put it at the lowest, religion must have served a useful function in the experience of the human species. It has been a universal factor in the life of nations, and when one form has decayed it has revived in another form; and this seems to be conclusive evidence that it has at least been advantageous to man in adapting him to his environment, and seconding his efforts after self-protection and self-expansion. . . .

2. I observe in the next place that the sublimity of the doctrines in which religious thought culminated creates a well-founded pre-possession in favour of their truth. Religious thought, like the universe, is on the grand scale. At its highest reach it has been a magnificent handling of a magnificent theme.

The idea of God in its matured form is a contribution to Theoretical Philosophy of the first magnitude. It is in fact the greatest idea which is at the disposal of the mind when it seeks to understand and interpret existence as a whole, and to build up an Ontology. For this purpose two other ideas are available—to wit, the world and the self; but the idea of God far surpasses both since it incorporates the elements to which each owes its dignity, and at the same time exalts them to the degree which is appropriate to the all-perfect Being. . . . The idea of God, moreover, makes it possible to embrace the totality of existence in a satisfactory view, and to organize knowledge of its structure and contents by reference to one supreme principle. . . .

3. The next step in the argument is that the truth of religion is vouched for by the self-evidencing power with which it has laid hold on the human mind. The most obvious reason why religion has been believed by man is, as Coleridge put it, that it found him, or, in Bosanquet's phrase, that he felt that this was the real thing. And the reason was a good one.

WILLIAM PATERSON PATERSON, Glasgow, 1924-5, *The Nature of Religion*, pp. 473, 475-6, 481.

90

The Justification of Belief

A man believes in God before he can say why he believes in God, but he will not go on believing in God, if, being a rational man, he has brought the belief into connexion with other knowledge about the universe and convinced himself that it is incompatible with some bit of Reality of which he is certain. If, however, after bringing his belief in God into connexion with other knowledge about the Universe, he finds the hold of the belief upon him unrelaxed, he will be able to point to grounds which seem to justify his belief. He will be able 'to give a reason for the faith that is in him'.

It is highly improbable that anyone who had no belief in God was ever led to believe in God by any of the standard 'proofs' of God's existence—the ontological, cosmological, teleological proof. They were thought of by men who already believed in God as considerations harmonizing their belief, for themselves, and for others, with a general view of the universe. It is, of course, a dogma of the Roman Church that the existence of God can be demonstrated by rational inference from visible phenomena. But no Roman Catholic could take this to mean that it can be demonstrated by arguments which are sure to be recognized by all men of normal understanding as cogent, for it is a plain fact of the world that there are many men of normal understanding who do *not* recognize the arguments put forward as cogent. Nobody who believes the dogma could take it in any other sense than that the arguments *ought to be* recognized as cogent, that if people were perfectly rational they would recognize them as cogent. If you already believe in God, then you will see everything that exists as existing because of the one Will which called the world into being, and so the cosmological argument will indicate this rational agreement between your belief and your view of the universe: you will see the order of the universe as directed to realize value in a supreme degree, and so the teleological argument will indicate rational agreement between your belief and your view of the universe. It is only, I think, in the sense of giving rational comfort to people who already believe in God that the standard arguments can be regarded as demonstrating the existence of God. What actually causes anyone to believe in God is a direct perception of the Divine.

EDWYN BEVAN, Edinburgh, 1933-4, *Symbolism and Belief*, pp. 344-5.

91

The Validity of Religious Experience

Religious experience is an emotional and conative attitude towards the whole of being, which is groundless and irrational unless a psychical life answering to it, as its appropriate object, really pervades and controls the universe, including the individual who feels it. Such an attitude differs profoundly from the merely aesthetic, inasmuch as in its full development it involves the entire nature of man, aesthetic, theoretic and practical—his entire outlook on the whole of which he is a member. Now those who have this religious experience find it a ground for believing in the reality of its object; a ground which cannot be stated in any formal argument, and cannot therefore be communicated to one who does not sufficiently share in the experience itself which is its source. The belief thus arising may indeed be disturbed and even, it may be, upset by difficulties and objections. But apart from such counter-motives, the religious experience carries conviction in proportion as it is intense, comprehensive and persistent. In it is to be sought the most important ground which has actually led mankind to believe in God.

What has the philosopher to say concerning the validity of this ground? Let us be clear on one point from the outset. We cannot translate the evidence of the religious experience into any formal argument without missing precisely what gives it its distinctive cogency. We cannot, for instance, argue that because men feel in a certain way therefore there is a God. If the religious experience is really cogent, its peculiar cogency can be appreciated only in actually experiencing it, not in any external description or definition of it.

On the other hand, there is a question which the philosopher can and ought to regard as falling within his own province—the question whether, on critical reflexion, we can find good reasons for regarding this sort of evidence as fallacious. If there are no such reasons—if, on the contrary, we find reason for regarding it as a sort of evidence which may be or ought to be cogent—then it is unchallenged, and there is no ground for rejecting it as invalid.

GEORGE FREDERICK STOUT, Edinburgh, 1919-21, *God and Nature*, pp. 255-6.

92

Question and Answer

The existential question, namely man himself in the conflicts of his existential situation, is not the source for the revelatory answer formulated by theology. One cannot derive the divine self-manifestation from an analysis of the human predicament. God speaks to the human situation, against it, and for it. Theological supra-naturalism, as represented, for example, by contemporary neo-orthodox theology, is right in asserting the inability of man to reach God under his own power. Man is the question, not the answer. It is equally wrong to derive the question implied in human existence from the revelatory answer. This is impossible because the revelatory answer is meaningless if there is no question to which it is the answer. Man cannot receive an answer to a question he has not asked. (This is, by the way, a decisive principle of religious education.) Any such answer would be foolishness for him, an understandable combination of words—as so much preaching is—but not a revelatory experience. The question asked by man is man himself. He asks it, whether or not he is vocal about it. He cannot avoid asking it, because his very being is the question of his existence. In asking it, he is alone with himself. He asks 'out of the depth', and this depth is he himself.

The truth of naturalism is that it insists on the human character of the existential question. Man as man knows the question of God. He is estranged, but not cut off, from God. This is the foundation for the limited right of what traditionally was called 'natural theology'. Natural theology was meaningful to the extent that it gave an analysis of the human situation and the question of God implied in it. One side of the traditional arguments for the existence of God usually does this, in so far as they elucidate the dependent, transitory, and relational nature of finite human existence. But, in developing the other side of these arguments, natural theology tried to derive theological affirmations from the analysis of man's finitude. This, however, is an impossible task. None of the conclusions which argue for the existence of God is valid. Their validity extends as far as the questioning analysis, not beyond it. For God is manifest only through God. Existential questions and theological answers are independent of each other.

PAUL TILLICH, Aberdeen, 1953-4, *Systematic Theology*, Vol. 2, pp. 14-15.

93

The Existential Moment of Faith

It is the paradox of the Christian message that the eschatological event, according to Paul and John, is not to be understood as a dramatic cosmic catastrophe but as happening within history, beginning with the appearance of Jesus Christ and in continuity with this occurring again and again in history, but not as the kind of historical event which can be confirmed by any historian. It becomes an event repeatedly in preaching and faith. Jesus Christ is the eschatological event not as an established fact of past time but as repeatedly present, as addressing you and me here and now in preaching.

Preaching is address, and as address it demands answer, *decision*. This decision is obviously something other than the decisions in responsibility over against the future which are demanded in every present moment. For in the decision of faith I do not decide on a responsible action, but on a new understanding of myself as free from myself by the grace of God and as endowed with my new self, and this is at the same time the decision to accept a new life grounded in the grace of God. In making this decision I also decide on a new understanding of my responsible acting. This does not mean that the responsible decision demanded by the historical moment is taken away from me by faith, but it does mean that all responsible decisions are born of love. For love consists in unreservedly being for one's neighbour, and this is possible only for the man who has become free from himself.

It is the paradox of Christian being that the believer is taken out of the world and exists, so to speak, as unworldly and that at the same time he remains within the world, within his historicity.

RUDOLF BULTMANN, Edinburgh, 1954-5, *History and Eschatology*, pp. 151-2.

94

A Paradox

The proofs are ineffectual precisely when they would be most necessary, when, that is, it is a question of convincing an unbeliever; conversely, when belief is already present and when, accordingly, there is the minimum of agreement, then they seem to serve no useful purpose. If a man has experienced the presence of God, not only has he no need of proofs, he may even go so far as to consider the idea of a demonstration as a slur on what is for him a sacred evidence. Now from the point of view of a philosophy of existence, it is this sort of testimony which is the central and irreducible datum. When, on the other hand, the presence of God is no longer—I shall not say felt, but recognized, then there is nothing which is not questionable. . . . The truth seems to be that there is room for only one thing here, and that is a conversion which no creature can flatter himself he is capable of bringing about. There is hardly any phrase which is more detestable than 'so and so has *made* so many conversions'. It amounts to dragging conversion to the level of a piece of magic. Spiritually speaking such a comparison is outrageous. This, we have seen, is the domain of grace; it is also the domain of intersubjectivity, where all causal interpretations are a mistake.

GABRIEL MARCEL, Aberdeen, 1949-50, *The Mystery of Being*, Vol. 2, pp. 176-7.

95

Cannot You See it for Yourselves?

I have spoken of the Christian revelation as dovetailing into a hypothesis of natural theology. We must not forget that logically both have the same character. The one is the interpretation by human reason of the appearance of human beings and their history in the evolutionary process; the other is the interpretation by human reason of the appearance within that history of the events to which the Bible bears witness. Those of us to whom the latter, equally with the former, approves itself as apprehension of truth, do find in it some further light on the dark mystery of evil. We still have to walk more by faith than by sight. But light shines into the darkness from the faith that the mystery we seek to fathom springs from the intensity of our Creator's care for our freedom. Whether we walk by the path of philosophy, of theology or of religion, we draw near to our goal when we think of the ultimate reality not as It but Him of whom the prophet wrote: 'He said, Surely they are my people . . . so He was their Saviour, in all their afflictions He was afflicted.'

Here, if this Christian faith be true, we have discovered the sense in which the Bible is unique as a medium of God's self-revelation. It does not come from its writers having been inspired to surpass all other men in moral and spiritual insight, but from the fact that the events to which they bore witness were those in which God was surmounting the difficulties inherent in His will to create genuinely free beings. If in theological language we call this His redemptive, as distinct from His creative, activity, we must be careful not to press the distinction so as to think of it as an afterthought, a remedy devised to recover from 'a divine fiasco'. The will to create persons endowed with genuine freedom includes within it the will to remedy their misuse of it in such a way as not to set aside but to set forward their growth in true freedom. The Christian gospel is the proclamation that actually, in the history of this world, God has been at work, and is still at work, doing this. We are not to proclaim this gospel either as derived from a guaranteed manual of doctrinal information or as a theory issuing from the minds of men specially endowed with religious genius. We are to proclaim it as the true interpretation of a series of events, starting with the story of Abraham, continuing in that of the children of Israel, culminating in the coming of Christ and issuing in the history of the Christian Church. If we want to commend it to others we have to do what we do in all spheres of discussion: we have to explain how we see the evidence and ask, 'Cannot you see it for yourselves?'

LEONARD HODGSON, Glasgow, 1955-7, *For Faith and Freedom*, Vol. 2, pp. 63-4.

96

Religious Tolerance

The fundamental positive motive for toleration is a recognition of the truth that religious conflict is not just a nuisance but is a sin. It is sinful because it arouses the wild beast in Human Nature. Religious persecution, too, is sinful because no one has a right to try to stand between another human soul and God. Every soul has a right to commune with God in God's and this soul's way; and the particular way concerns none but God and the particular soul in question. No other human being has a right to intervene by the use of any means except non-violent missionary action. And Violence in this field is not only sinful; it is futile; for religions cannot be inculcated by force. There is no such thing as a belief that is not held voluntarily through a genuine spontaneous inner conviction. Different people's convictions will differ, because Absolute Reality is a mystery of which no more than a fraction has ever yet been penetrated by—or revealed to—any human mind. 'The heart of so great a mystery cannot ever be reached by following one road only.'[1] However strong and confident may be my conviction that my own approach to the mystery is a right one, I ought to be aware that my field of spiritual vision is so narrow that I cannot know that there is no virtue in other approaches. In theistic terms this is to say that I cannot know that other people's visions may not also be revelations from God—and these perhaps fuller and more illuminating revelations than the one that I believe that I myself have received from Him.

. . . All human beings who are seeking to approach the mystery in order to direct their lives in accordance with the nature and spirit of Absolute Reality or, in theistic terms, with the will of God—all these fellow-seekers are engaged in an identical quest. They should recognize that they are spiritually brethren and should feel towards one another, and treat one another, as such. Toleration does not become perfect until it has been transfigured into love.

ARNOLD TOYNBEE, Edinburgh, 1952-3, *An Historian's Approach to Religion*, pp. 250-1.

[1] Quintus Aurelius Symmachus, in a controversy with Saint Ambrose.

VIII
JUST AS ASTRONOMY
OR CHEMISTRY

I wish the lecturers to treat their subject as a strictly natural science, the greatest of all possible sciences, indeed in one sense, the only science, that of Infinite Being. . . . I wish it considered just as astronomy or chemistry is.

Just as Astronomy or Chemistry

Lord Gifford wished the subject to be treated as a strictly natural science, just as astronomy or chemistry is. But *natural* obviously is only opposed here to *supernatural*, only to what concerns Revelation. . . . If it were said that astronomy is to be treated as a strictly natural science just as chemistry is, would it be necessary to substitute in the former the method of the latter—to roast Jupiter in a crucible, or distil Saturn over in a retort? . . . The apparatus of chemistry is for chemistry, and the apparatus of astronomy is for astronomy; neither can be substituted for the other; and both are powerless in regard to the object of Natural Theology. Our transatlantic brothers, as we hear at this moment, are going to have object glasses, or reflectors, or refractors, of ever so many feet; but the very tallest American, with the very tallest of telescopes, will never be able to say that he spied out God. Natural Theology is equally known as Rational Theology; and Rational Theology is equally known as the Metaphysic of God. The last phrase is acceptable enough; it repugns not; but fancy the Physic of God! The Greek term, doubtless, has an identity with the Latin one; but it has also a difference. Natural Theology may be considered a strictly natural science; but it were hardly possible to treat it as a strictly physical science. *Physical* Theology sounds barbarous, and carries us no farther than Mumbo-Jumbo and the fetich in general.

JAMES HUTCHISON STIRLING, Edinburgh, 1888-90, *Philosophy and Theology*, pp. 32-3.

Just as Astronomy or Chemistry?

Theology, as Aristotle saw, is truly that in which all philosophy culminates: for theology alone regards existence in its totality—if indeed the term 'totality' may be applied to what is infinite. Theology is infinite in its scope: astronomy and chemistry concentrate themselves upon selected portions of what is finite.

Therefore, when theology is (perhaps misleadingly) called 'natural', and when Gifford lecturers are enjoined to treat this subject as 'a strictly natural science', I am obliged to infer that the important adjective 'natural' does not mean that Infinite Being, the object of study and inquiry, is to be included in nature—unless the ambiguous word 'nature' is used in an all-comprehensive meaning, and not as a synonym for things and persons evolved in time. It is the visible phenomena within this system that natural sciences, such as astronomy and chemistry, are employed in seeking for and interpreting. In the narrower meaning of 'nature' the 'Infinite Being' of natural theology is *super*natural; and 'natural' theology is concerned with what is supernatural or metaphysical. The implied analogy between the theology that is 'natural', and sciences like astronomy and chemistry, must, therefore, mean something different from their being all concerned at last with natural causes.

I conclude, accordingly, that the intended meaning of 'natural' in Lord Gifford's deed, is found more fully in the next injunction: 'I wish the lecturers to treat their subject . . . without reference to, or reliance upon, any supposed special, exceptional, or so-called miraculous revelation'. That means, I suppose, that, just as 'astronomy and chemistry'—the two named examples of 'natural' science—must be formed by methodical observation of events in nature, and freely formed inferences founded thereon—so, the theology which is 'natural' must be determined by facts, and by principles of reason known to be true in their own light—not dogmatically assumed, on the infallible authority of a Church, or of books assumed to express infallibly the divine purpose. We know that there is no such dogmatically imposed authority for an infallible astronomy, or an infallible chemistry, which would supersede rational investigation. In like manner, blind reliance on supposed infallibility, biblical or traditional, in matters of religious thought, must be put aside by the Gifford lecturer; so that all the three sciences—the two physical ones now named and the unique science of the Universal Power—must alike make their final appeal to reason in experience; not to traditional authority *per se*, which can never be the *final* court of appeal for a reasonable being, on any question natural or supernatural. What is meant seems to be, that *reasonableness* must finally direct us, in this as in everything else, if we are reasonable beings.

ALEXANDER CAMPBELL FRASER, Edinburgh, 1894-6, *Philosophy of Theism* (2nd ed), pp. 17-18.

How and Why

Knowledge of the why, even were it possible, could in no sense dispense us from seeking the how—and that is all that concerns science . . . but, if anyone looks only for the how, can he be surprised if he fails to find the why?

ETIENNE GILSON, Aberdeen, 1931-2, *The Spirit of Medieval Philosophy*, p. 105.

Scientific Method

In the natural sciences progress may be made in two ways: one by deducing results from ascertained principles, the other by framing hypotheses suggested no matter how, though usually by some observed phenomenon, and trying whether they will so link together observed phenomena as to force on us a conviction of their truth. . . .

In a similar way we may conceive that progress may be made in natural theology in either of two ways: by deducing consequences from what we know or observe, or by assuming *for trial* the truth of a statement made on whatever authority it may be, and then examining whether the supposition of its truth so falls in with such knowledge as we possess, or such phenomena as we observe, as to lead us to a conviction that the statement does indeed express the truth. It may be that the statement comes from a source which professes to be a revelation made from God to man. But such an employment of it as I have just described is strictly analogous to our procedure in the study of physical science, and does not therefore seem to be precluded by the terms of the foundation of this lectureship.

GEORGE GABRIEL STOKES, Edinburgh, 1891-3, *Natural Theology*, Vol. 1, pp. 2-3.

Obiter Dicta on the Nineteenth Century

Among other things, our science (of religion) has demonstrated by historical and psychological research that the religious need is a general human need. And the more we study religion, the further we penetrate into its history, the better we understand the nature of its doctrines, so much the more clearly we shall see that it is entitled to precedence in our spiritual life, because the religious need is the mightiest, profoundest, and most overmastering of all. Let no dread of ecclesiastical ambition and sacerdotal tyranny prevent us from recognizing this; for they are powerless except when true religion languishes or slumbers. Once awaken religion to full life and activity, and their influence is gone. Will it now reawake?

Our brilliant nineteenth century has achieved wonders, but it has been disappointed in its expectation of such a reawakening. The waning century seems weary and almost despairing. It sometimes speaks of the bankruptcy of science and the illusions of philosophy.

CORNELIUS PETRUS TIELE, Edinburgh, 1896-8, *Elements of the Science of Religion*, Vol. 2, pp. 261-2.

The Jig-Saw Puzzle of Science

Scientific discovery is like the fitting together of the pieces of a great jig-saw puzzle; a revolution in science does not mean that the pieces already arranged and interlocked have to be dispersed; it means that in fitting on fresh pieces we have had to revise our impression of what the puzzle-picture is going to be like. One day you ask the scientist how he is getting on; he replies, 'Finely. I have very nearly finished this piece of blue sky.' Another day you ask how the sky is progressing and are told, 'I have added a lot more, but it was sea, not sky; there's a boat floating on top of it.' Perhaps next time it will have turned out to be a parasol upside down; but our friend is still enthusiastically delighted with the progress he is making. The scientist has his guesses as to how the finished picture will work out; he depends largely on these in his search for other pieces to fit; but his guesses are modified from time to time by unexpected developments as the fitting proceeds. These revolutions of thought as to the final picture do not cause the scientist to lose faith in his handiwork, for he is aware that the completed portion is growing steadily. Those who look over his shoulder and use the present partially developed picture for purposes outside science, do so at their own risk.

ARTHUR STANLEY EDDINGTON, Edinburgh, 1927, *The Nature of the Physical World*, pp. 352-3.

103

The Elephant on the Hillside

Let us then examine the kind of knowledge which is handled by exact science. If we search the examination papers in physics and natural philosophy for the more intelligible questions we may come across one beginning something like this: 'An elephant slides down a grassy hillside. . .'. The experienced candidate knows that he need not pay much attention to this; it is only put in to give an impression of realism. He reads on: 'The mass of the elephant is two tons'. Now we are getting down to business; the elephant fades out of the problem and a mass of two tons takes its place. What exactly is this two tons, the real subject matter of the problem? It refers to some property or condition which we vaguely describe as 'ponderosity' occurring in a particular region of the external world. But we shall not get much further that way; the nature of the external world is inscrutable, and we shall only plunge into a quagmire of indescribables. Never mind what two tons *refers* to; what *is* it? How has it actually entered in so definite a way into our experience? Two tons *is* the reading of a pointer when the elephant was placed on a weighing-machine. Let us pass on. 'The slope of the hill is 60°.' Now the hillside fades out of the problem and an angle of 60° takes its place. What is 60°? There is no need to struggle with mystical conceptions of direction; 60° is the reading of a plumb-line against the divisions of a protractor. Similarly for the other data of the problem. The softly yielding turf on which the elephant slid is replaced by a coefficient of friction, which though perhaps not directly a pointer reading is of kindred nature. . . .

And so we see the poetry fades out of the problem, and by the time the serious application of exact science begins we are left with only pointer readings. If then only pointer readings or their equivalents are put into the machine of scientific calculation, how can we grind out anything but pointer readings? But that is just what we do grind out. The question presumably was to find the time of descent of the elephant, and the answer is a pointer reading on the seconds' dial of our watch.

ARTHUR STANLEY EDDINGTON, Edinburgh, 1927, *The Nature of the Physical World*, pp. 251-2.

104

Science and Religion

In spite of their relations, science and religion remain, and must remain, distinct. If there were no other way of establishing a rational order between things than that of reducing the many to the one, either by assimilation or by elimination, the destiny of religion would appear doubtful. But the struggles which contrasts engender admit of solutions other than those which science and logic offer. When two powers contend, both of them equally endowed with vitality and fertility, they develop and grow by that very conflict. And, the value and the indestructibility of each becoming more and more evident, reason thrives to bring them together through their conflicts, and to fashion, from their union, a being richer and more harmonious than either of them taken apart.

Thus it is with religion and science. Strife tempers them both alike; and, if reason prevails, from their two distinct principles—become, at once, wider, stronger, and more flexible—will spring a form of life ever ampler, richer, deeper, freer, as well as more beautiful and more intelligible. But these two autonomous powers can only advance towards peace, harmony, and concord, without ever claiming to reach the goal; for such is the human condition.

ÉMILE BOUTROUX, Glasgow, 1903, *Science and Religion in Contemporary Philosophy*, pp. 399-400.

Science and Philosophy

It is true the development of the common sea-urchin seems at the first glance rather remote from the concept of categories and morality and universal teleology, and thus it might seem, as many modern philosophers maintain, as if science and philosophy were really two things, only loosely connected.

But there were philosophers in former times—and among them were Leibniz and Hegel—who did not take such a short-sighted view. And I think they are right.

Givenness is One and philosophy is the endeavour to understand Givenness. Part of Givenness is sensations, part of it is categories, part of it is feeling, part of it is memory, and there are many other parts. The domain of Givenness which is formed out of sensations and categories we call Nature. It makes no logical difference, it seems to me, whether nature is studied with regard to what it actually is, that is to say, what really happens in it, or whether we try to discover which elemental parts of our mental organization come into play in conceiving nature and what 'nature' means in the sphere of metaphysics.

The first is generally called science and the latter philosophy.

But in the last resort there is only one kind of human knowledge.

HANS DRIESCH, Aberdeen, 1907-08, *The Science and Philosophy of Organism*, Vol. 2, pp. 374-5.

Scepticism of Scepticism

Keeping in mind the intrinsic stability of the concepts of natural language in the process of scientific development, one sees that—after the experience of modern physics—our attitude toward concepts like mind or the human soul or life or God will be different from that of the nineteenth century, because these concepts belong to the natural language and have therefore immediate connection with reality. It is true that we will also realize that these concepts are not well defined in the scientific sense and that their application may lead to various contradictions, for the time being we may have to take the concepts, unanalysed as they are; but still we know that they touch reality. It may be useful in this connection to remember that even in the most precise part of science, in mathematics, we cannot avoid using concepts that involve contradictions. For instance, it is well known that the concept of infinity leads to contradictions that have been analysed, but it would be practically impossible to construct the main parts of mathematics without this concept.

The general trend of human thinking in the nineteenth century had been toward an increasing confidence in the scientific method and in precise rational terms, and had led to a general scepticism with regard to those concepts of natural language which do not fit into the closed frame of scientific thought—for instance, those of religion. Modern physics has in many ways increased this scepticism; but it has at the same time turned it against the overestimation of precise scientific concepts, against scepticism itself. The scepticism against precise scientific concepts does not mean that there should be a definite limitation for the application of rational thinking. On the contrary, one may say that the human ability to understand may be in a certain sense unlimited. But the existing scientific concepts cover always only a very limited part of reality, and the other part that has not yet been understood is infinite. . . . We know that any understanding must be based finally upon the natural language because it is only there that we can be certain to touch reality, and hence we must be sceptical about any scepticism with regard to this natural language and its essential concepts. Therefore, we may use these concepts as they have been used at all times. In this way modern physics has perhaps opened the door to a wider outlook on the relation between the human mind and reality.

WERNER HEISENBERG, St Andrews, 1955-6, *Physics and Philosophy*, pp. 171-3.

107

Docility and Adventurousness

It seems to me, then, that the rightful demand of the intellect for individual freedom to think sincerely and fearlessly, and the equally rightful demand of religion for objectivity and protection against the vagaries of pure subjectivity, can only be harmonized in one way, through the cultivation, by all parties who are concerned that human life shall be the prey neither of worldliness nor of superstition, of the two complementary qualities of docility and adventurousness. In the past untold mischief has been wrought by their separation. The *ecclesia docens*, the official body of teachers in the religious community, has often shown a high degree of adventurousness in its bold formulations of articles of faith, or other propositions claiming to embody the content of what is authoritative; from the rest of the community it has demanded unqualified submissiveness. Or, in reaction to this demand, individual thinkers have denied the right of authority, reposed in any external body, to exercise any control over, or receive any deference from, the solitary mental adventurer. Indeed, not so long ago, there seemed to be, at least in Western Europe, a still more complete inversion of the parts played for so many centuries by the *ecclesia docens* and the individual. We have witnessed something hardly to be distinguished from a claim on the part of self-constituted representatives of the secular sciences to be the sovereign authority which dictates but does not obey, while official theologians have, in large numbers, been almost comically anxious to show their docility by accepting almost any speculation put before the British Association by a Professor, or a Fellow of the Royal Society, or communicated to the newspapers by a medical man of any notoriety, as the latest deliverance of an infallible authority, to which religion must at once conform itself, at its peril. Neither the ends of pure religion, nor the purposes of sound science are well served by these attempts to make authoritarian dictation the duty, or privilege, of one set of men and teachable humility that of another. No man will be either a true saint or a man of the right scientific temper who does not know how to be at once docile and adventurous in his own personal thinking.

ALFRED EDWARD TAYLOR, St Andrews, 1926-7, *The Faith of a Moralist*, Vol. 2, pp. 225-6.

108

The God of Science

Scientific speculation, in so far as it leads to a God, leads merely to One Whose will is the cause of events. We infer that He is the Mind from

Whose creative activity all that lies behind phenomena derives such reality as it possesses. We may thus reach, though we cannot go much further than, a somewhat colourless Deism or pantheism unless we pass beyond the boundaries of scientific enquiry.

It would, however, be wrong to imply that such scientific enquiry is without its own values. It is truth supreme; and thus the God inferred from science is intolerant of falsehood and superstition. There is, moreover, an aesthetic element in scientific theory. The mathematician shapes his symbols and polishes his formulae until they take to themselves a satisfying beauty. Thus the God inferred from science has a power which is both harmonious and beautiful: He is not some rough uncouth giant, though such a being would be fit to represent the psychical aspect of the blind forces of Nature. Nevertheless, though all values are not excluded from the realm of scientific enquiry, the fact remains that good and evil find no place in scientific schemes; and therefore no arguments strictly based upon such schemes can lead to a God Whose goodness draws us to Himself. Yet unless we can think of God as a Father, responsive to our struggle to overcome evil and ready to aid us by some measure of communion with Himself, He is not the object of religious aspiration but merely the end of a limited range of speculative enquiry.

ERNEST WILLIAM BARNES, Aberdeen, 1927-9, *Scientific Theory and Religion*, pp. 599-600.

109

Religion is not threatened

Religion is not threatened. Although certain religious views may conflict with scientific facts, religion itself is not endangered by any legitimate result of scientific research, by any utterance of true art, or by any philosophical or ethical system thoughtfully based on sound principles. On the contrary, all this promotes the growth of religion, compelling it to remould antiquated forms, which injure it by clinging to old errors, and to bring them into harmony with the needs of the age.

CORNELIUS PETRUS TIELE, Edinburgh, 1896-8, *Elements of the Science of Religion*, Vol. 2, p. 259.

Nature's Harmony

One thing we can discern about nature . . . at least it is a harmony. Now that the magical has been exorcised from it we can feel the vast unbroken harmony it is. Where tragedy and where comedy and where both it is at least a harmony all its own. That we should have attained that knowledge, that it should be given us to apprehend that, that we can follow its being that, can hear it, trace it, retrace it in part and even forecast it as such, is an inexpressibly estimable good. We are privileged in this. It is, so far as we detect, uniquely the possession of ourselves—it is *the* human possession. . . . It is the old primeval gift of knowledge, which we, wiser now, know was not primeval but is of yesterday—therefore with promise of further. We traced how, it would seem, we are so fashioned that our world, which is our experience and is one world, is a diune world, a world of outlook and inlook, of the experienced perceptible and of the experienced imperceptible. This world with all its sweep of content and extent taxes utterance to indicate. Yet it is given us in so far to seize it, and as one coherent harmony. More; it is revealing to us the 'values', as Truth, Charity, Beauty. Surely these are compensation to us for much. And will not this compensation grow? Charity will grow; Truth grows; and even as Truth so Beauty. Music as her ear grows finer embraces what once were discords. The mind which began by being one thing has truly—as so often in evolution—gone on to being another thing. Even should mind in the cataclysm of Nature be doomed to disappear and man's mind with it, man will have had his compensation: to have glimpsed a coherent world and himself as an item in it. To have heard for a moment a harmony wherein he is a note. And to listen to a harmony is to commune with its Composer?

CHARLES SHERRINGTON, Edinburgh, 1937-8, *Man on His Nature*, pp. 400-01.

III

The Limitations of Science

To abandon religion for science is merely to fly from one region of faith to another, from one field of ignorance and conjecture to another.

It is best to forget what science said yesterday if you are to believe what she says today.

Logic does not help you to appreciate York Minster, or Botticelli's *Primavera*, and mathematics give no useful hints for lovers.

You cannot draw conclusions about the universe from the inspection of a six-acre field.

WILLIAM MACNEILE DIXON, Glasgow, 1935-7, *The Human Situation*, pp. 46, 56, 64, 94.

II2

A Biological Heretic

You will see that I am a biological heretic. I believe that the living world is as closely linked with theology as it is with physics and chemistry: that the Divine element is part of the natural process—not strictly super-natural, but para-physical.

It has been the great success of physical science—so much easier to investigate with our bodily senses and the extensions we invest to aid them—which for the last 300 years has excited attention and tended to push the study of the psychic side of life into the background. I believe that a truer biology, one that will not sell its soul to physics and chemistry for quick results, will emerge and tackle the more important and more difficult aspects of life about whose nature we are almost as ignorant as when physics and chemistry began. I say more important because in this field lie consciousness, the nature of memory, the feeling of purpose, love, joy, sorrow, the sense of the sacred, the sense of right and wrong, the appreciation of beauty—indeed all the things that really matter in life. Some of them, of course, are likely always to lie in the field of natural history rather than of science. Natural theology will extend from science, through natural history to religion.

I shall shock some of my colleagues when I say that I sometimes feel a sympathy for Shaw's elderly gentleman in *Back to Methuselah* who said, 'They tell me there are leucocytes in my blood and sodium and carbon in my flesh. I thank them for the information and tell them there are black beetles in my kitchen, washing soda in my laundry and coal in my cellar. I do not deny their existence but I keep them in their proper place.' We must keep physics and chemistry to their proper proportions in the scheme of life.

ALISTER HARDY, Aberdeen, 1963-5, *The Living Stream*, p. 284.

113

Lost—One Key

The key we seem to have lost is just the key to human nature. Religion has at all times claimed to possess this key. Even the agnostic who doubts the claim as raised by religion will probably have to admit that it would be vital for us to have an adequate understanding of human nature. All the troubles I mentioned before do not arise out of an insufficient mastery of the powers of the physical world; they arise out of our inability to conduct, to predict or even to understand the actions of human beings. Now to deny that science makes important contributions to such an understanding would again be wrong. But besides admitting the limitations of our scientific knowledge of the human heart we have to understand the highly ambiguous poten-tialities of the power implied in such knowledge. The idea that the psychological insight of a Freud might be combined in one man with the purposes and cunning of a Goebbels will make us shudder. Pavlov's study of conditioned reflexes seems to be the historical origin of the method now called brainwashing. Scientific knowledge means power. Power ought to mean responsibility. But that scientific knowledge would supply us with the ethical greatness needed to bear this responsibility is a hope not warranted by the facts. I think it can be stated bluntly that scientism, if it rests its trust on the expectation that science by its own nature is enabled to give us sufficient guidance in human affairs, is a false religion. Its faith, if going so far, is superstition; the role of the priest does not become the scientist and good scientists know that; the scientific code of behaviour needs a background of an ethics which science has not been able to provide.

CARL FRIEDRICH VON WEIZSACKER, Glasgow, 1959-61, *The Relevance of Science*, pp. 22-3.

IX

SO-CALLED MIRACULOUS REVELATION

I wish the lecturers to treat their subject as a strictly natural science . . . without reference to or reliance upon any supposed special, exceptional or so-called miraculous revelation.

Cain's Wife

In our large towns in these days, in our capitals, in our villages, we are confronted by a vast mass of unbelief. The Aufklärung, the historical movement called the Aufklärung, as I say, dead among thinkers, has descended upon the people; and there is hardly a hamlet but has its Tom Paines by the half-dozen—its Tom Paines of the tap, all emulously funny on the one subject. I witnessed such a thing as this myself last summer in the country—the bewildered defeat of my landlady under the crowning triumph of her son, a lad of seventeen or so, who had asked her to explain to him where Cain got his wife!

. . . He, now, who would boggle at the wife of Cain, or stumble over the walls of Jericho, is not an adult: he is but a boy still. For my part, I do believe—I feel sure—that David Hume, that Voltaire himself were he alive now, and were he cognizant of all the education that we have received since, even on prompting of his own, would not for a moment be inclined to own as his these laggards and stragglers of an army that has disappeared. He would know that the new time had brought a new task, and he would have no desire to find himself a mere anachronism, and historically out of date.

JAMES HUTCHISON STIRLING, Edinburgh, 1888-90, *Philosophy and Theology*, pp. 15-16, 19.

Natural Theology aud Miraculous Revelation

The note of naturalness in theology . . . lies in its superiority to restrictions due to special historic conditions. The antithesis of natural is not to revealed: but to one type of revealed, exalted as the alone revealed, to the exclusion of all others. When it uses the term 'natural', it does not, except in the restricted sense of physico-theology, mean to exclude from its survey the field of history and of human life. It rejects, indeed, the notion of special revelation, if that be understood to imply the communication of full-made truths by a miraculous importation of them into human faculties. But, on the other hand, it does not, by calling itself natural or rational, imply that it turns its back on history and experience. It may be that in certain epochs, in a fit of disgust at vulgar credulity and in hatred of superstition, it imagined that un-assisted reason could of itself construct a creed. But in so far as it did so, it was labouring under an illusion. There is no absolutely unassisted reason. Reason, on the contrary, only lives by a perpetual antithesis to sense: it only emerges from the soil of reality and life, from the fact of experience: it is experience made more and more harmonious, complete and self-explanatory. Its only conflict with revelation arises because revelation is said to introduce into the sphere of human knowledge and experience a fact absolutely unique and incommensurable. Unique and incommensurable in a way, every reality is: but not in the sense that it forms no part in the compass of reality, giving to and taking from its environment. Natural theology, the theology of reason, claims the prerogative of man to examine all things, and is but an attempt in a special range of questions to carry out that purpose fully, without bar or check from any specially privileged province.

WILLIAM WALLACE, Glasgow, 1893-4, *Lectures and Essays on Natural Theology and Ethics*, pp. 22-3.

116

General and Special Revelation

While greatly preferring the distinction between a general and special revelation to the traditional one between a natural and a revealed knowledge, I cannot find it wholly satisfactory. Not all the light that God has imparted to the various pagan peoples in the course of their historical experiences is general to them all; there is something that is special to each. It is for these reasons that I feel, like not a few of my predecessors, somewhat baffled by Lord Gifford's wish that his lectures should proceed 'without reference to or reliance upon any supposed special, exceptional, or so-called miraculous revelation'.

JOHN BAILLIE, Edinburgh, 1961-2, *The Sense of the Presence of God*, p. 188.

117

A False Distinction?

The notion that there is one set of truths, such as the existence and providence of God, the principles of morality, and the natural immortality of the soul, which we can accept on the testimony of reason, and another set of truths, the peculiar doctrines of the Gospel, which we must accept, if at all on the testimony of revelation, is for Christian thought futile and impossible. The truths of natural religion, in so far as they are contained in Christianity, are not contained therein simply by addition or accretion, but rather by absorption and transmutation.

JOHN CAIRD, Glasgow, 1892-3 and 1895-6, *The Fundamental Ideas of Christianity*, Vol. 1, p. 21.

118

Natural Theology and Revealed Religion

Any divorce between natural theology and revealed religion is, in my opinion, to be deprecated. In the study of natural theology we are not to shut our eyes to such light as may be thrown on the subject by revealed religion, or to refuse to entertain for trial some solution of a difficulty felt by natural theology on the ground that the solution in question involves the supernatural. On the other hand, in the study of revealed religion we are not to reject the exercise of moral faculties in forming our judgment as to whether what is asserted to be revealed is really so, and is rightly interpreted.

GEORGE GABRIEL STOKES, Edinburgh, 1891-3, *Natural Theology*, Vol. 2, p. 258.

Revelation and Reason

In one of his early works, *Problems in the Relation of God and Man*, published in 1911, Dr C. C. J. Webb gave the quietus to the two-source theory of knowledge. He showed that the traditional division of truth into that which may be discovered by human reason, and that which must be accepted from divine revelation, cannot be maintained on either side. If God be the God of the first article of the Nicene Creed: 'Maker . . . of all things visible and invisible', all discoveries in the field assigned to human reason are discoveries about God as He makes Himself known in His handiwork. We cannot think that man is able to discover truths about God as it were behind God's back, nor can we approve the intellectual pelagianism in the idea that there is a field within which man can discover truth without divine assistance. On the other hand, it would be no use for God to give revelations to creatures incapable of receiving them, and the only way in which truth can be received is by a mind that can distinguish between truth and falsehood, in other words, by the exercise of reason. Revelation and reason are not alternatives appropriate to different fields of inquiry. They are correlative, the divine and the human sides involved in all man's growth in knowledge.

LEONARD HODGSON, Glasgow, 1955-7, *For Faith and Freedom*, Vol. 1, p. 80.

All Existence is Revelation

We affirm, then, that unless all existence is a medium of Revelation, no particular Revelation is possible; for the possibility of Revelation depends on the personal quality of that supreme and ultimate Reality which is God. If there is no ultimate Reality, which is the ground of all else, then there is no God to be revealed; if that Reality is not personal, there can be no special revelation, but only uniform procedure; if there be an ultimate Reality, and this is personal, then all existence is revelation. Either all occurrences are in some degree revelation of God, or else there is no such revelation at all; for the conditions of the possibility of any revelation require that there should be nothing which is not revelation. Only if God is revealed in the rising of the sun in the sky can He be revealed in the rising of the son of man from the dead; only if He is revealed in the history of Syrians and Philistines can He be revealed in the history of Israel; only if He chooses all men for His own can He choose any at all; only if nothing is profane can anything be sacred. It is necessary to stress with all possible emphasis this universal quality of revelation in general before going on to discuss the various modes of particular revelation; for the latter, if detached from the former, loses its root in the rational coherence of the world and consequently becomes itself a superstition and a fruitful source of superstitions. But if all existence is a revelation of God, as it must be if He is the ground of its existence, and if the God thus revealed is personal, then there is more ground in reason for expecting particular revelations than for denying them.

(*The whole of this passage is printed in italics.*)

WILLIAM TEMPLE, Glasgow, 1932-4, *Nature, Man and God*, pp. 306-7.

121

Continued Revelation

Does God continue to reveal himself to mankind? A little boy is reading his lesson in Bible history: 'And God said unto Moses.' His critical younger brother, who has not yet begun to go to school: 'What a stupid you are! God can't speak in that way to a man.' 'Shut up, he could in those days.' Does not theology reason much in the same way?

In certain later writings of the Old Testament and in Judaism piety no longer discerns the action of God in the present history and its personalities—with less difficulty, it is true, in his wise and great works in nature—but, as regards history, only in the ancient wonders of revelation. . . .

But that it is absurd to look upon God's Revelation as finished with

Christ or the Bible, is clearly shown by another question. Our question: 'Does God continue to reveal himself to mankind?' gives rise to another question. 'Did God ever reveal himself to mankind?' I am anxious to emphasize this question, which lurks behind our topic. It makes evident how impossible it is to realize and to maintain the conviction of a real Revelation of God without applying it also to the present time. Take somebody who does not believe in any working of God; take a man for whom the Living God does not exist; how are you to convince him of the existence of a God who has once revealed himself to mankind, if God does not reveal himself to that man as living and working in his salvation? But there are pious people who believe in God not only as a law and principle, or as a great all-pervading mystery, but as a Will, as Love, that had made itself known and perceptible to man, yet who consider that the Revelation in a proper sense was finished with Christ or with the Bible. . . .

Our Christian faith and our constructive outlook on life and history know something more. They know that God works in the complicated course of generations, and that the right man is there to do his work, when he is wanted.

NATHAN SODERBLOM, Edinburgh, 1931, *The Living God*, pp. 350-1, 355.

122

Miracle and Natural Science

The decay of the belief in miracles which has taken place progressively in modern times is undoubtedly due in large part to the progress of Natural Science, with the emphasis which it places upon order or uniformity in phenomena. It must however be distinctly recognized that there exists, and can exist, no *a priori* proof of the impossibility of what are called miracles. If that impossibility has been sometimes asserted by exponents of Natural Science, the assertion is merely a piece of *a priori* dogmatism, quite incapable of substantiation on scientific grounds. We have no *a priori* knowledge of what can, and what cannot, occur in Nature. We have only presumptions, psychologically explicable as expectations due to habits of thought founded on our past experience. The decay of belief of which I have spoken depends in large part upon a change of attitude towards an unusual or unexpected occurrence, and also consists in large part of a more critical attitude towards the evidence that such alleged events have actually occurred. To the modern man of science, an event which does not appear to happen in accordance with known laws is an occurrence which suggests to him the inadequacy of those laws, or the presence of some disregarded factor. He is incited to attempt, by means of the extension of known laws, to subsume the occurrence under a more complete set of laws, or to determine the character of the particular disturbing factor which had in the first instance been left out of account. What would perhaps formerly have been regarded as a miracle is, for the modern man, not a case of breach of order, but an occasion for extending his knowledge of it.

ERNEST WILLIAM HOBSON, Aberdeen, 1921-2, *The Domain of Natural Science*, pp. 490-1.

123

Emergent Evolution and Miracle

According to emergent evolution we find and loyally accept a series of ascending steps in advance as we pass from natural entities of lower to those of higher status; and in the evolution of that which we deem the highest of natural entities, a man, these steps afford instances of a determinate plan which includes the evolutionary progress of all relevant events in him, alike in physical and in mental regard. But someone may say: There is yet another regard. What you regard as emergent steps in advance I, for my part, regard as miracles. Each miracle is new and unpredictable on the basis of the order of nature *as known up to date*. In this sense it cannot be other than an instance of supernatural intervention directive of the order of natural events. And what you regard as the comprehensive and determinate plan of events, I cannot but regard as Divine Purpose within which each several miracle has contributory place.

It seems, then, that the same array of facts may afford instances of determinate plan in naturalistic regard and of Divine Purpose in religious or spiritual regard. And if this be so there need not be any discrepancy. Naturalistic interpretation may be supplemented by spiritual explanation without any savour of contradiction.

I say that there *need* be no discrepancy, and that naturalistic interpretation *may be* supplemented by spiritual explanation. But here much turns on what we understand by 'supernatural intervention'. If it imply ultimate and ineradicable dualism then I think we must say that any monistic interpretation, such as I advocate, cannot be other than false.

. . . But within one order of reality there cannot be two orders of reality—the one called natural and the other called supernatural. I must therefore state frankly that in rejecting dualism, even in our present context, I reject also what is meant by supernatural *in this sense.* There is for me . . . one and only one realm of reality that *is both natural and spiritual*, in ultimate unity of substance, but *is not both natural and supernatural* if this imply ultimate diversity of orders of being.

CONWY LLOYD MORGAN, St Andrews, 1922-3, *Life, Mind and Spirit*, pp. 300-2.

124

A Progressive Enterprise

The acceptance of the Christian faith does not express the assertion of observable facts and consequently you cannot prove or disprove Christianity by experiments or factual records. Let me apply this to the belief in miracles. Ever since the attacks of philosophers like Bayle and Hume on the credibility of miracles, rationalists have urged that the acknowledgment of miracles must rest on the strength of the factual evidence. But actually, the contrary is true: if the conversion of water into wine or the resuscitation of the dead could be experimentally verified, this would strictly disprove their miraculous nature. Indeed, to the extent to which any event can be established in the terms of natural science, it belongs to the natural order of things. However monstrous and surprising it may be, once it has been fully established as an observable fact, the event ceases to be regarded as supernatural. Recent biological suggestions, for example, that virgin birth *might* take place in exceptional circumstances would, if accepted as the explanation of the birth of Christ, not confirm, but totally destroy the doctrine of the Virgin Birth. It is illogical to attempt the proof of the supernatural by natural tests, for these can only establish the natural aspects of an event and can never represent it as supernatural. Observation may supply us with rich clues for our belief in God; but any scientifically convincing observation of God would turn religious worship into an idolatrous adoration of a mere object, or natural person.

Of course, an event which has in fact never taken place can have no supernatural significance; and whether it has taken place or not must be established by factual evidence. Hence the religious force of biblical criticism, shaking or, alternatively, corroborating certain facts which form the main themes of Christianity. But evidence that a fact has not occurred may sometimes leave largely unimpaired the religious truth conveyed by a narrative describing its occurrence. The book of Genesis and its great pictorial illustrations, like the frescoes of Michelangelo, remain a far more intelligent account of the nature and origin of the universe than the representation of the world as a chance collocation of atoms. For the biblical cosmology continues to express—however inadequately—the significance of the fact that the world exists and that man has emerged from it, while the scientific picture denies any meaning to the world, and indeed ignores all our most vital experience of this world. The assumption that the world has some meaning which is linked to our own calling as the only morally responsible beings in the world, is an important example of the supernatural aspect of experience which Christian interpretations of the universe explore and develop. . . .

Christianity is a progressive enterprise. Our vastly enlarged perspectives of knowledge should open up fresh vistas of religious faith. The Bible and the Pauline doctrine in particular, may still be pregnant with unsuspected lessons; and the greater precision and more conscious flexibility of modern thought, shown by the new physics and the logico-philosophic movements of our age, may presently engender conceptual reforms which will renew and clarify, on the grounds of modern extra-religious experience, man's relation to God. An era of great religious discoveries may lie before us.

MICHAEL POLANYI, Aberdeen, 1951-2, *Personal Knowledge*, pp. 284-5.

125

Hume, Spinoza and Leibniz on Miracles

David Hume argued that miracles must be impossible to prove, at least so far as their evidence depends on history and tradition; because faith in individual testimony can never be as credible as the cosmic faith that every event must have a natural cause: human experience of the uniformity of the physical evolution is more credible than any historic record of its non-uniformity can be: witnesses are found fallible, but the course of nature is never found fallible; and even if an infallible witness could be produced, when pitted against the infallible natural order, the contradiction between the two infallibles could only produce sceptical paralysis of all faith, into which a thinker, baffled by what is self-contradictory, inevitably subsides. . . .

Spinoza's argument for the impossibility of miracles may be taken as expressing the common scientific difficulty. The system of nature, it is by implication argued, must be already perfect, if it is divine. Its occasional miraculous modification would imply its imperfection; for what is always perfectly good does not admit of being altered and mended by an afterthought. To admit a miracle is to admit finite imperfection in divinely natural law; it also implies inconstancy or caprice, not the divine perfection which leaves no room for amended thoughts. What is already perfect does not permit of improvement by occasional miracle. . . .

But do we know enough about the office of the physical system in the economy of the universe to justify the assumption that issues cannot appear in the material world, or in a human mind, independently of any *physical law* of God in nature that can never be construed in science; yet without contradicting or interrupting any of those laws? 'I hold,' says Leibniz, 'that when God works miracles He does it, not in order to supply the wants of *nature*, but those of *grace*; and whoever thinks otherwise must have a very mean notion of the wisdom and power of God.' Occasional miracles may be in that case divine acts, proper to a universe that includes persons or moral agents; while they would be out of place in a universe of things, wholly under mechanical relations.

ALEXANDER CAMPBELL FRASER, Edinburgh, 1894-6, *Philosophy of Theism* (2nd edn), pp. 295, 301, 303.

126

All Life is Revelation

Theologians have assumed that the ordinary visible world is simply the physically interpreted world, even though this world is also assumed to have been originally created. As a consequence it can only be through what is supernatural that God, as the source of spiritual values, is revealed to us, since spiritual values are without meaning in a physically determined world. Thus a supernatural element seems to be essential for religion. Revelation becomes also a supernatural process, but for which we should be in the presence of only a natural world of mere mechanism. When the true nature of the materialism in ordinary theology is recognized, there is no need for a supernatural element in religion. To insist on the need for it becomes equivalent to insistence on doubting the omnipotence and omnipresence of God. No supernatural revelation is needed, because conscious behaviour contains within itself the revelation of God's existence and nature.

In current theology our knowledge of the existence of God is treated as a revelation made only at certain times and places. We must accept it in this sense or leave it. An attempt is also made to support the supposed revelation by arguments based on supposed design in the apparent physical world, or supposed existence of supernatural events in this apparent world. These arguments are simply a buttressing of bad theology by bad science. The real evidence for God's existence and love is within and around us everywhere and at all times when we take from our eyes the scales of bad philosophy or theology which obscure our vision.

When we understand the real evidence that this universe is nothing but a spiritual universe and the manifestation of God present within and all around us, the Churches can again teach, in a manner which will carry general conviction, these old words which have brought strength to go forwards, peace of mind, and charity, to so many: 'For I am persuaded that neither death, nor life, nor angels, nor principalities, not powers, nor things present, nor things to come, nor height, nor depth, nor any other creature, can separate us from the love of God.

JOHN SCOTT HALDANE, Glasgow, 1927-8, *The Sciences and Philosophy*, pp. 291-2, 340.

X

OBLIGATIONS AND DUTIES

Natural Theology in the widest sense of that term . . . the Knowledge of God . . . the Knowledge of the Relations which men and the whole universe bear to Him, the Knowledge of the Nature and Foundation of Ethics or Morals, and of all Obligations and Duties thence arising.

127

The Fundamental Question

Our western philosophy began with the breakdown of a way of life in ancient Greece, which posed the question 'What should we do?' If it has found itself driven to dwell almost exclusively with the sister question 'How can we know?' it remains true that this question is incomplete in itself; and that the complete question, in the end, is 'How can we know what we should do?'

JOHN MACMURRAY, Glasgow, 1953-4, *The Self as Agent*, pp. 23-4.

128

The Destiny of Man

The lower stages of evolution seem unworthy of the Creator, but when we think of man with his reason and conscience as latent therein, it becomes conceivable how the Divine Spirit might brood yearningly over chaos, starting the mighty movement by which it was to be slowly turned into a cosmos with man for its crown of glory. Evolution does not degrade man, man confers honour on evolution. Man, considered as in his whole being the child of evolution, instead of being a stumbling-block to faith, is rather the key to all mysteries, revealing at once the meaning of the universe, the nature of God, and his own destiny.

ALEXANDER BALMAIN BRUCE, Glasgow, 1897-8, *The Providential Order of the World*, p. 48.

Tribal Morality and Religion

The virtues fostered by clan-religion are, naturally, those which make for the cohesion of the group and its efficiency in war, which is a permanent feature of existence for these small wandering clans—obedience, endurance, courage, loyalty, and unhesitating self-sacrifice to the common cause. . . . The scope of primitive morality and primitive religion does not extend beyond the limits of the clan or tribe: stranger and enemy are synonymous terms, and no considerations of humanity intervene to mitigate the ferocity of intertribal warfare. But narrow as is the range of tribal morality and religion, its importance as a stage on the way to higher things can hardly be over-rated. 'First, the blade, then the ear, then the full corn in the ear.' The habits formed by the discipline of the clan, the virtues nourished by the sense of kinship, formed the natural seed-ground of the larger morality which embraces all mankind. The development of the one into the other is the history of human progress. . . . Hence even in its rudest forms religion was a moral force. Instead of being a noxious and superfluous after growth, according to the Enlightenment and Free-thought theory, religion is from the first, as Hegel called it, the bearer (*Träger*) of human civilization.

ANDREW SETH PRINGLE-PATTISON, Edinburgh, 1922-3, *Studies in the Philosophy of Religion*, pp. 58-9.

130

The Derogation of Action

The depreciation of action, of doing and making, has been cultivated by philosophers. But while philosophers have perpetuated the derogation by formulating and justifying it, they did not originate it. They glorified their own office without doubt in placing theory so much above practice. But independently of their attitude, many things conspired to the same effect. Work has been onerous, toilsome, associated with a primeval curse. It has been done under compulsion and the pressure of necessity, while intellectual activity is associated with leisure. On account of the unpleasantness of practical activity, as much of it as possible has been put upon slaves and serfs. Thus the social dishonour in which this class was held was extended to the work they do. . . .

It is probably in consequence of the derogatory view held of practice that the question of the secure place of values in human experience is so seldom raised in connection with the problem of the relation of knowledge and practice. But upon any view concerning the status of action, the scope of the latter cannot be restricted to self-seeking acts, nor to those of a prudential aspect, nor in general to things of expediency and what are often termed 'utilitarian' affairs. The maintenance and diffusion of intellectual values, of moral excellencies, the aesthetically admirable, as well as the maintenance of order and decorum in human relations are dependent upon what men do.

Whether because of the emphasis of traditional religion upon salvation of the personal soul or for some other reason, there is a tendency to restrict the ultimate scope of morals to the reflex effect of conduct on one's self. . . . The idea that the stable and expanding institution of all things that make life worth while throughout all human relationships is the real object of *all* intelligent conduct is depressed from view by the current conception of morals as a special kind of action chiefly concerned with either the virtues or the enjoyments of individuals in their personal capacities.

JOHN DEWEY, Edinburgh, 1929, *The Quest for Certainty*, pp. 8-9, 32-3.

131

Liberty, Creativity, Responsibility

Here, then, is our trinity of notions, our libertarian battlecry, Liberty, Creativity, Responsibility—or death! We are free, and free to make our lives, but always in response to claims: claims which we may be psychologically free, but are not morally free, to ignore. What is it, then, that ultimately exerts these claims upon us? The philosophy of 'How we think' may point out with complacency that we do not commonly trace our responsibilities to a higher source than the custom of our kind, or cite an authority superior to the American way of life. And doubtless a Gallup poll, say of the Civil Service and other black-coated workers, would do much to support the contention; especially if the questionnaire were suitably framed. *Vox Gallupi vox Dei*; still, we must be careful not to misinterpret so august an oracle. It may be that people are content to find their authority in custom; but authority for what? Not, ultimately, for what they should do, but for what they should prize. The man who follows the American way of life does not see in the customs of the tribe obligatory performances, which are their own justification; he takes them both to express, and to be inspired by, a respect for humanity.

. . . . We may respect the American way of life as a sound indicator, pointing out to us what there is in humanity most deserving of respect, as well as how that respect may in practice be paid. Humanity we respect absolutely, if once we can see it straight; and this respect obliges us; we hold ourselves responsible for acting, or failing to act, in accordance with it.

We say that our respect is payable to humanity. The word is almost too convenient; indeed, to the modern ear it is an actual equivocation. It means mankind, and it means the characteristic excellence of human nature. Both are objects of respect, or of regard. But so far from coinciding in practice, they are inclined to tug us in different directions, and, on occasion, to tear us apart. To regard mankind is to accept men as they are, to spare them frustration, to give them their will and pleasure. To regard humanity, in the other sense, is to look for what a believer calls the divine image in us, and the unbeliever the human ideal.

AUSTIN FARRER, Edinburgh, 1957, *The Freedom of the Will*, pp. 301-2.

132

The Nature of Ethics

Ethics is often described as a normative science, as laying down norms or rules of right or of good behaviour. That seems to me to be in a sense true, and in a sense untrue. In a sense, ethics would be guilty of great officiousness in undertaking this task. There are many plain men who already know as well as any moral philosopher could tell them, how they ought to behave. Not only do they see their concrete duty, in the difficult situations of life, with admirable clearness and correctness, but they have principles, of a certain degree of generality, on which no moral philosopher can improve—tell the truth, keep your promises, aim at the happiness of those round you and so on. But these general principles, while perfectly sound when properly understood, are apt to lead to difficulties, familiar even to the plain man, when their nature is not properly understood; for they are apt to conflict, at least in appearance, with one another. . . .

Rules such as 'tell the truth', 'injure no man', cannot survive if they continue to be taken as absolute rules of such a kind that any and every act which is an instance of telling the truth is thereby rendered right, and any act which is an instance of injuring another man is thereby rendered wrong. The rules cannot *both* be true, when thus understood, if there is a single case in which one cannot tell the truth without inflicting pain. . . . The only way to save the authority of such rules is to recognize them not as rules guaranteeing the rightness of any act that falls under them, but as rules guaranteeing that any act which falls under them tends, so far as that aspect of its nature goes, to be right, and can be rendered wrong only if in virtue of another aspect of its nature it comes under another rule by reason of which it tends more decidedly to be wrong. Kant overshot the mark when he tried to vindicate for such rules absolute authority admitting of no exception; but he would have been right if he had confined himself to insisting that any act which violates such a rule must be viewed with suspicion until it can justify itself by appeal to some other rule of the same type.

WILLIAM DAVID ROSS, Aberdeen, 1935-6, *Foundations of Ethics*, pp. 311-13.

133

Duty

It is clear that it is always morally better to act from the sense of duty than to do an alternative act from any other motive, however good, and if the sense of duty is the best motive when it is in conflict with others, it is also the best motive when it conspires with others in pointing to the same action. It is best because, while the other good desires are desires to bring into being this or that good thing, without considering whether it is the greatest good one could bring about, in conscientious action an attempt, at least, has been made to do this.

While the desire to do one's duty is thus different in kind from all other motives, it seems true to say, not, with Kant, that it alone has moral value, but that it has the highest moral value. Certain other motives also have moral value, because of the affinity of nature that there is between them and the sense of duty, since they include a part of the thought which is included in the sense of duty. The other good motives are attractions towards certain actions *as being of a certain character*; the sense of duty is an attraction towards them *as being right as being possessed of that same character.*

Again, it does not seem to be correct to say, with Kant, that the addition of any other motive to the sense of duty necessarily makes the motive of the act less good than it would be without that addition. So long as the strength of the sense of duty is equal in both cases, the addition of another good motive improves the motivation, and the addition of a neutral motive, i.e. of the desire for one's own happiness, does nothing to make the motivation worse.

Motive is the main factor that makes an action good or bad, but it is not the only one. . . . The motive of an act of self-sacrifice may be no better than that of another in which no self-sacrifice is involved; but the former action includes also the intention to accept pain to ourselves as the price we are ready to pay to bring about the good we desire to bring about; and, our own pleasure being morally neutral, willingness to give it up in a good cause is a component which has moral worth and gives additional worth to the action that involves it.

WILLIAM DAVID ROSS, Aberdeen, 1935-6, *Foundations of Ethics*, pp. 325-7.

134

The Categorical Imperative

The categorical imperative is an absolute *thou shalt*; it implies absolute devotion. And the realm of nature will not provide us with any absolute. It can provide the finite alone, for nature is the realm of finitude. The experience of duty as something with an absolute claim upon us implies a belief in the infinite. I appeal to the experience; the defence of the categorical imperative as the summit of morality, propounded by Kant has never been so effectively upheld as by Professor Paton whose *Categorical Imperative* has never been answered, let alone refuted. But, assuming the experience of this imperative, and its moral worth, what does it involve and imply? In the first place it is reasonable; we would not be ourselves if we did not hear and obey the call which is binding on us, not as creatures of nature or as sufferers, but as thinkers. Secondly it would be foolish to seek knowledge if it were not to be had or to be scientists if the universe were not intelligible. Our quest for truth implies that we believe in the intelligibility of nature, so that, as I have urged earlier, the universals are implicit within it waiting to be actualized by becoming known. And the same is true of morality. Either we are deluded or else we live in a moral world, a world not alien to a moral quest. And we cannot reasonably say that we are deluded here, because if we were deluded here we would be deluded everywhere. Truth would be as unattainable as moral worth. The quest for truth and the call of duty both involve absolute claims, and the absoluteness is there, faintly, in ourselves as the call of ourselves, as self-conscious agents and thinkers, to realize more completely this presence of the infinite within our finitude. Moral advance, like the advance of knowledge, is the discovery of reality.

Confronted with a duty we are confronted with something absolute which we are constrained to obey, although in obeying we find ourselves perfectly free, free from nature, free in the life of reason, free in the service of the ideal. Mere knowledge of the ideal will not produce action but only contemplation. I have tried to describe how we rise from desires for we know not what, to rational choice. We do not leave desire behind, but it becomes a desire for the fulfilment of the higher self. We are conscious of a tension between what we are and what we might be, and this produces the desire to make ourselves different and better. But this happens only because the ideal is not purely transcendent; it is partly realized in us already.

MALCOLM KNOX, Aberdeen, 1966-8, *Action*, pp. 240-1.

135

The Rational Man

Rationality, as we conceive it, does not lie merely in letting reason appoint one's beliefs, hard as that is; it means carrying a rational spirit into the ramifications of practice, making it permeate one's feelings and pervade the decisions of one's will. It means to be a practising philosopher. This is a very much harder business than being a mere professor of philosophy. For it requires being what professors of philosophy so seldom are, reasonable men who live rational lives. Indeed if one's picture of the rational man had to be drawn from the flesh, one would search for a model in vain. He has never, in fact, existed, and can only be imagined. We do know, however, that he would fall somewhere between two extremes, and in trying to see what he is like, we may find it suggestive to begin with what he is certainly not.

At one extreme, then, stands the creature of impulse whose only principle is to have no principle, who surrenders to the mood of the hour, whatever that may be. He will do nothing unless at the moment his heart is in it; to be forced by himself or others into acting against his feelings seems to him slavery; freedom means following impulse. . . .

At the other extreme stands what Lord Russell was no doubt referring to when he spoke of 'that inhuman monster "the rational man"'. . . . He tries to incarnate pure intelligence. The wheels of his intellect revolve in a vacuum, and if at a furious pace, so much the better. He acts always from calculation, never from impulse, affection, or even hatred. He sees a long way ahead, cunningly adjusts his means to his ends, is all things to all men while caring little for any, never forgets himself, and is never carried away by enthusiasm, or sentimentality. While making no mistakes of his own, at least none that mere intelligence could avoid, he sees through everyone else, notes their stupidities, and uses them with superlative craft for his own purpose. He is icily competent, intimidatingly efficient, free from all romantic and humanitarian nonsense, knows what he wants, and moves toward it by the straightest line. . . .

He will be far, then, from the crafty monster, with ice-water in his veins, that romantics have sometimes pictured. Unless he were capable of feeling and impulse, there would be nothing that his intelligence could present to him as worth pursuing. He will have his enthusiasms and loves and hates like other men, and will translate them—not precipitately or rashly, indeed, but judiciously—into action.

BRAND BLANSHARD, St Andrews, 1951-3, *Reason and Goodness*, pp. 409-12.

136
What is a Good Man?

A man who is intent on doing good is often called *benevolent*. A man can be a 'benefactor' without being benevolent, e.g. if he does good to others mainly for the sake of promoting his own social prestige. A true benefactor must be a man who does good (to others), but he need not be that which is ordinarily called a good man.

I am not suggesting that there is a common and important use of the phrase 'a good man' to mean the same as 'a benevolent man'. But I think it is true to say that when the phrase 'a good man' is used with a so-called moral meaning, it is *related* to our idea of a benevolent man. It is of some interest in this connexion to notice that the opposite to a benevolent man, i.e. a malevolent man or a man who is intent on doing evil or mischief, is quite commonly and naturally also called, in a moral sense, 'a bad man'.

One affinity between the morally relevant notion of a good man and the notion of a benevolent man is in any case that both notions have to do with features of human *character*. A man may do some bad acts and even entertain some evil intentions—and yet be a good man. But the bad he does or intends must count as an occasional aberration. Or it must have some special excuse. If we were asked how much evil the good man can be 'allowed', we could, of course, not answer by giving an exact measure—'hereunto and no further'. But we could give an inexact and yet significant measure by saying that the bad he does or intends must not affect our judgment of his character. A good man may do some mischief, or revenge a wrong which he has suffered from another man, or tell a lie. But he cannot be mischievous or revengeful or untruthful.

With this last remark we are also touching upon one of the differences between goodness and benevolence as attributes of men. A benevolent man is not necessarily a virtuous man, and he may be lacking in a sense of justice. Virtue and justice are two prominent features in our picture of moral excellence.

GEORG HENRIK VON WRIGHT, St Andrews, 1958-60, *Varieties of Goodness*, pp. 134-5.

137

Love is of God

All truth must be God's, as has been said, intuitively or without the discursive process by which the human understanding mostly works: so that truth may be said to belong to his nature, whereas for man it is

167

something to be attained. Something similar holds true when we speak of the love of God. By moralists love has been regarded as the crowning feature of the virtuous life, and theologians have reached no more profound definition than that God is love. Can it be said that the two qualities—the human love and the divine—are only connected by an uncertain analogy? It is true that love, as used of God, does not connote all that it habitually does in its human manifestations, while on the other hand it must at the same time connote much more. But it does in both cases mean the will to the good of others and the will to communion with them. The good which love seeks is not in either case merely happiness, but rather in the first place the realization in each person of the values of which he is capable. And the communion which love seeks will be facilitated by agreement as to the values most cherished. Love is possible as a one-sided relation only; but the communion in which it finds satisfaction is a reciprocal relation. Communion with God is therefore possible only when man's nature is purged from lower desires and his affections set on the things that are more excellent. Only the pure in heart can see God and hold communion with him. Thus the love of God is a will to the good of men which has as its end the communion of man with God, and it is manifested in the secular process whereby the soul is turned from things of sense to spiritual interests and is thus fitted for citizenship in the kingdom of God.

WILLIAM RITCHIE SORLEY, Aberdeen, 1914-15, *Moral Values and the Idea of God*, pp. 498-9.

138

Values and Action

Only a child in the degree of his immaturity thinks to settle the question of desirability by reiterated proclamation: 'I want it. I want it, I want it.' What is objected to in the current empirical theory of values is not connection of them with desire and enjoyment, but failure to distinguish between enjoyments of radically different sorts. There are many common expressions in which the difference of the two kinds is clearly recognized. Take for example the difference between the ideas of 'satisfying' and 'satisfactory'. . . . That it is satisfying is the content of a proposition of fact; that it is satisfactory is a judgment, an estimate, an appraisal. It denotes an attitude *to be* taken, that of striving to perpetuate and to make secure.

It is worth notice that besides the instances given, there are many other recognitions in ordinary speech of the distinction. The endings 'able', 'worthy' and 'ful' are cases in point. Noted and notable, noteworthy; remarked and remarkable; advised and advisable; wondered at and wonderful; pleasing and beautiful; loved and lovable; blamed and blameable, blameworthy; objected to and objectionable; esteemed and estimable; admired and admirable; shamed and shameful; honoured and honourable; approved and approvable; worthy of approbation, etc. The multiplication of words adds nothing to the force of the distinction. But it aids in conveying a sense of the fundamental character of the distinction; of the difference between mere report of an already existent fact and judgment as to the importance and need of bringing a fact into existence. The latter is a genuine practical judgment, and marks the only type of judgment that has to do with the direction of action. Whether or no we reserve the term 'value' for the latter (as seems to me proper) is a minor matter; that the distinction be acknowledged as the key to understanding the relation of values to the direction of conduct is the important thing.

JOHN DEWEY, Edinburgh, 1929, *The Quest for Certainty*, pp. 247-9.

139

Value

One can generally tell a man's special field of investigation by the words which he uses carefully and the words he uses carelessly. The physicist now uses the word 'atom' carefully; that is, he is prepared to say what he means by it. The geneticist is careful with such words as 'heredity' and 'environment'; the theologian with the word 'god'. . . . The philosopher who is engaged in that branch of philosophy now known as 'theory of value' is distinguished by the fact that the word he is most careful about is the word 'value'.

Everyone else uses this word carelessly. . . . 'Value' is now a favourite word among the sociologists, psychologists, and psychiatrists. The word is scattered through the text, and even mentioned in the index; but it is used like 'and', 'but', and the nouns and adjectives of everyday speech, as though its meaning were so well understood as to require no examination. The theorist of value, on the other hand, is one who asks, of himself and of others, 'Precisely what is meant by "value"?' It is his business to have an answer to that question. In other words, 'value' is his *careful* word.

According to the definition of value here proposed, a *thing—any thing —has value, or is valuable, in the original and generic sense when it is the object of an interest—any interest. Or, whatever is object of interest is ipso facto valuable.* Thus the valuableness of peace is the characteristic conferred on peace by the interest which is taken in it, for what it is, or for any of its attributes, effects, or implications.

Value is thus defined in terms of interest, and its meaning thus depend on another definition, namely, a definition of interest. The following is here proposed: interest is *a train of events determined by expectations of its outcome. Or, a thing is an object of interest when its being expected induces actions looking to its realization or non-realization.* Thus peace is an object of interest when acts believed to be conducive to peace, or preventive of peace, are performed on that account, or when events are selected or rejected because peace is expected of them.

RALPH BARTON PERRY, Glasgow, 1946-8, *Realms of Value*, pp. 1-3.

140

Equality

From whatever point of view we consider the progress in enlightenment or in the conception of the moral ideal from the more primitive to the more advanced peoples, it seems to take the form of an increasing recognition of the fundamental importance of personality and of the distinction between persons and things. Increasingly accurate knowledge of matters of fact, and increasing communications and contacts and co-operation between individuals and peoples, provide conditions in which moral insight can function more effectively; and, as it does so, we find men slowly, intermittently and haltingly, but none the less surely, coming to recognize other men as persons, independent, responsible, self-governing individuals. Things we try to master and control and use. Their value consists in ministering to our purposes. Persons are subjects of purposes, not just objects of the purposes of other people. They are separate centres of spiritual life, independent expressions of the moral consciousness. This characteristic of men as persons is what . . . the advanced religions refer to when they say that all men are equal in the sight of God.

This moral equality of men is, of course, compatible with many differences between them in other respects. Men differ in physical and mental capacity, in knowledge and experience, in wisdom and moral goodness, and so on; but they are equal in a sense which is deeper than all their differences. They are all subjects not objects, persons not things, ends not means. They are self-conscious moral beings, having in themselves a principle of self-government which gives them a worth and dignity which entitle them to our consideration and respect. Only as we recognize this do we understand them as they really are.

ALEXANDER MACBEATH, St Andrews, 1948-9, *Experiments in Living*, pp. 451-2.

141

Christian Morality

Christian morality has developed, is developing, and will develop. It will not have attained completeness until experience has ceased to revise, correct, and supplement tradition. Science teaches with authority within its own sphere, and Christian morality, just because it is Christian, cannot ignore or resist its teaching. But history, in recording the development of Christian morality, has disclosed the singular character of that development, as always ultimately determined by certain vital ideas or principles which were confessedly paramount in the life and teaching of Jesus, and which have in the sphere of personal character perpetuated His influence. This original determining factor has guaranteed identity through the mutations of Time, and tends to assert itself more effectively as mankind is carried on the stream of evolving process out of aboriginal savagery to the height of modern civilization. This factor, the specifically Christian factor, gives distinctive character to the civilization of Christendom.

Christian morality is religious morality. It assumes that 'the spirit of man is the candle of the Lord', and, being thus indestructibly theistic, it provokes against itself the resolute hostility of all who repudiate religion.

HERBERT HENSLEY HENSON, St Andrews, 1935-6, *Christian Morality*, pp. 313-14.

142

The 'Third Way'

Of course Christianity has failed in supporting a kind of patriarchism and paternalism which, in a technical world, could not but work out in autocracy and economic tyranny. But the Church is supremely right in affirming that the family pattern is the Christian pattern of all social life. What needs to be seen is that the family pattern needs to be worked out in our day in quite new forms, doing justice to the legitimate claim of each member of the family to personal dignity and basic independence.

It is here that the Christian Church has a great task to fulfil. The Christian conception of man stands above the false alternative of individualistic liberalism or capitalism and collectivistic State Socialism or Communism. Christianity is absolutely unique in presenting a conception of man in which true personality and true community are not only firmly connected with one another but, at bottom, identical. Wherever a community is firmly grounded in Christian thinking, neither individualistic capitalism nor collectivist Communism or State-Socialism are possible. The 'third way' is inherent in the Christian conception of man itself. That is why Christianity is called upon to lead the way wherever the third way is seen as necessary and wherever, out of economic life itself, new schemes of social order emerge which are neither individualistic nor collectivist.

At present collectivism is in the ascendent and individualism is on the wane. Christianity has the historical task of raising her voice against the great dangers for human personality as well as for community implied in the collectivist scheme.

EMIL BRUNNER, St Andrews, 1947-8, *Christianity and Civilization*, Vol. 2, p. 97.

172

Release from Evil

Religion requires us to accept as the will of God whatever evil comes upon us. Why, then, do we feel sure that we ought to diminish evil so far as we can, natural as well as moral, and that this is a religious duty? If God overrules it all, why should we interfere? The answer, it seems, must be that our interfering, so far as it is wise and good, is itself part of the process of overruling, it is a stage in the way by which the contradiction of the finite passes into harmony in the infinite. We are not something independent and apart from God. He does not—to use religious language—reconcile the world with himself by some process wholly outside the finite spirits, but in them. The completion of this process is beyond us; but we experience and take part in a stage of it. We help to will evil away. Only this 'we' is only 'we' so far as our will is God's. The faith by which the world is overcome and evil becomes the instrument of good is itself the action of God in overruling evil. Religion is release from evil because there is nothing in religion which is not divine as well as human.

ANDREW CECIL BRADLEY, Glasgow, 1907-08, *Ideals of Religion*, p. 284.

The Moral Argument—The Coping-Stone

It (the ontological argument) is, of course, not an argument at all, but rather a postulate, or, if you will, an intuition; in fact, a vote of confidence in reason passed by the philosopher before he proceeds to the order of the day. In any case, it does not conclude to the God of religion. Professor Dawes Hicks seems to me to have rendered a great service to religious philosophy when he presents, in his recently published *Hibbert Lectures*, the cosmological, teleological and moral arguments as grades in a hierarchical order, the first providing the groundwork for the second, and the second for the third. The cosmological argument proceeds from the fact that nature is not a self-contained and self-explicable system, reducible without remainder to law, to infer a necessary being above and beyond nature as the ground of its contingency. Of the two alternatives, an accidental world or a world dependent on a transcendent author, reason must needs prefer the latter. The teleological argument, which, while it does not *prove*, yet possesses a much higher degree of probability than Hume and Kant would allow, helps to bridge the gulf between a necessary being and a purposive intelligence. How can there be such a thing as purposiveness without a purposing mind? But intelligence is one thing, goodness another; for all that these two lines of inference tell us, the transcendent mind might work for evil or ethically neutral ends. To furnish an approach to the God of religion, there is required evidence of his goodness. The source of all being must also be the source of all value. In other words, rational theology finds its coping-stone in the moral argument.

WILLIAM GEORGE DE BURGH, St Andrews, 1938, *From Morality to Religion*, pp. 153-5.

XI

LIFE EVERLASTING

I give my body to the earth as it was before, in order that the enduring blocks and materials thereof may be employed in new combinations; and I give my soul to God, in Whom and with Whom it always was, to be in Him and with Him for ever in closer and more conscious union. . . . And my desire and hope is that these lectureships and lectures may promote and advance among all classes of the community the true knowledge of Him . . . Whom truly to know is life everlasting.

Immortality in the Ancient World

A mystic but not specially Orphic tone is heard in a Greek inscription found in a Sabine village, dating from the second century A.D. 'The Soul is immortal, for it came from God . . . the body is the garment of the Soul. Honour the God in me' (meaning the divine element). The Orphic dogma maintaining that the released soul enters upon a state of divinity . . . is more clearly revealed still in the few of the epitaphs collected. A certain Lucius dedicates a grave-monument to his four-year-old child in such strange words as these: 'To my sweetest child and personal God who hearkens to my prayers'. A priest of Thasos dedicates his deceased wife as 'an incarnate goddess'—Θεὰ ἐπιφανής. Similarly a dead man at Eruthrai is glorified as 'a blessed spirit that loves mankind, a new manifestation of Asklepios'. The fashion or the belief was taken over—as we have seen—by the Roman world; and a lady named Pomptilla, who died in Corsica to save her husband, is transfigured by him 'under the changed name of Juno and through all ages her fame will shine'.

LEWIS RICHARD FARNELL, St Andrews, 1920, *Greek Hero Cults and Ideas of Immortality*, p. 401.

The Ghost of a Ghost

Modern thought has deanthropomorphized what was left of anthropomorphic in religion, and, in the end, has left us for God, at most, 'a stream of tendency making for righteousness', or an energy unknown and unknowable—the ghost of a ghost. For the soul, by virtue of his belief in which man raised himself in his own esteem, and, more or less, in ethical standing, is left to us a negation or a wistful doubt.

ANDREW LANG, St Andrews, 1888-90, *The Making of Religion*, pp. 333-4.

Dying

In the face of the supreme mystery of death, primitive religion, from prehistoric times onwards, has by means of funeral rites given various expression to a steadfast faith in the reality of a future life. A certain conflict is to be noted between a fear of the contagion of death as represented by corpse or ghost and an affectionate desire to further the welfare of the departed in whatever abode he is supposed to dwell. On the whole, however, love prevails, and it is characteristic of the primitive community that it believes itself to be in friendly touch with ancestral spirits whose semi-divine powers are always at the disposal of the tribe if proper respect is paid to their wishes. Thus religion converts death itself into a source of hope and comfort.

ROBERT RANULPH MARETT, St Andrews, 1931-2, *Sacraments of Simple Folk*, p. 203.

Two Views

On the one hand, there are those who love to dwell on the grandeur and dignity of man, and who dwell with pride at the contemplation of the triumphs which his genius has achieved in the visionary world of imagination as well as in the realm of nature. Surely, they say, such a glorious creature was not born for mortality, to be snuffed out like a candle, to fade like a flower, to pass away like a breath. Is all that penetrating intellect, that creative fancy, that vaulting ambition, those noble passions, those far-reaching hopes, to come to nothing, to shrivel up into a pinch of dust? It is not so, it cannot be. Man is the flower of this wide world, the lord of creation, the crown and consummation of all things, and it is to wrong him and his creator to imagine that the grave is the end of all. To those who take this lofty view of human nature it is easy and obvious to find in the similar beliefs of savages a welcome confirmation of their own cherished faith, and to insist that a conviction so widely spread and so firmly held must be based on some principle, call it instinct or intuition or what you will, which is deeper than logic and cannot be confuted by reasoning.

On the other hand, there are those who take a different view of human nature, and who find in its contemplation a source of humility rather than of pride. . . . Those who take this view of the pettiness and transitoriness of man compared with the vastness and permanence of the universe find little in the beliefs of savages to alter their opinion. They see in savage conceptions of the soul and its destiny nothing but a product of childish ignorance, the hallucinations of hysteria, the ravings of insanity, or the concoctions of deliberate fraud and imposture. They dismiss the whole of them as a pack of superstitions and lies, unworthy the serious attention of a rational mind. . . .

Such are the two opposite views which I conceive may be taken of the savage testimony to the survival of our conscious personality after death. I do not presume to adopt the one or the other. It is enough for me to have laid a few facts before you. I leave you to draw your own conclusion.

JAMES GEORGE FRAZER, St Andrews, 1911-13, *The Belief in Immortality*, pp. 469-71.

149

'Where the Wicked Cease from Troubling . . .'

It is true that there is a gulf, wide and impassable, between the Babylonian religion as we decipher it in the cuneiform tablets, and the religion of Israel as it is presented to us in the Old Testament. On the one side, we have a gross and grotesque polytheism; on the other, an uncompromising monotheism. Babylonian religion made terms with magic and sorcery, and admitted them in a certain degree to its privileges; they were not incompatible with polytheism; but between them and the worship of the one God there could be no reconciliation. It was the same with the sensualities that masqueraded at Erech in the garb of a religious cult; they belonged to a system in which the sun-god was Baal, and a goddess claimed the divided adoration of man. To Israel they were forbidden, like the necromancy and witchcraft with which they were allied.

But deep and impassable as may be the gulf which separated the Mosaic Law from the official religion of Babylonia, different as may have been the development of prophecy in Babylonia and Israel, the primordial ideas from which they started were strangely alike. The same relation that is borne by the religion of ancient Egypt to Christianity is borne by the religion of Babylonia to Judaism. The Babylonian conception of the divine, imperfect though it was, underlay the faith of the Hebrew, and tinctured it up to the end. The Jew never wholly freed himself from the dominion of beliefs which had their first starting-point in the 'plain' of Babylonia; his religious horizon remained bounded by death, and the God of Abraham, Isaac, and Jacob continued to be the God of the living and not of the dead. It was in this world that the righteous were rewarded and the wicked punished; the world to come was the dreary shadow-land of Babylonian teaching, a land of darkness where all things are forgotten, but also a land where 'the wicked cease from troubling, and the weary are at rest'.

ARCHIBALD HENRY SAYCE, Aberdeen, 1900-02, *The Religions of Ancient Egypt and Babylonia*, pp. 500-1.

150

The Immortality of Mind

For once in the history of Greek thought religion, philosophy, and ethics are interfused. They all meet together in the Platonic doctrine of the Immortality of the Soul. The distinction of soul and body is sometimes regarded as a comparatively late development of human thought; but in one sense the separate existence of the soul is the most primitive of religious conceptions, and is implied in the earliest forms of sepulture. It had faded indeed into something very thin and shadowy for the age of Homer, but retained its vitality in central Greece, and had gained in warmth and intensity long before the time of Pindar and of

Aeschylus. The Orphic teaching and the Eleusinian mysteries had given a more distinct shape to yearnings never long absent from humanity, when becoming conscious of itself. What is peculiar to Plato is not the assertion of a life of the soul after death, but rather the identification of soul with mind. This places the idea of immortality on a new footing. For on the condition of the soul in its relation to truth and righteousness depends her state of blessedness now and hereafter. Hence Plato, while often treading, as his commentators affirm, in the footsteps of Orphic mysticism, regards with unmitigated abhorrence those ceremonial rites by which it was pretended that the soul could be purged from sin and satisfy offended gods. Such doctrines of redemption are to him abominable, for they imply an utterly unworthy notion of the moral nature of God.

LEWIS CAMPBELL, St Andrews, 1894-6, *Religion in Greek Literature*, pp. 350-1.

151

This is Life Eternal

When the Fourth Evangelist represents Jesus as saying 'This is life eternal, that they might know thee the only true God, and Jesus Christ, whom thou hast sent', he plainly does not refer to an immortality that is attained after death, but to a relationship here and now which does not change or pass away. He is, in fact, uttering what poets and mystics have always said, that in and through the transient is expressed and realized the permanent. If this be true—and there is a mass of testimony to it—then the antithesis between nature and supernature becomes absurd, and the total corruption of the natural must be abandoned: nature and grace become sacramentally related as outward to inward, and an incarnation of the divine is in keeping with the whole character of the physical world, since 'God so loved it'.

CHARLES EARLE RAVEN, Edinburgh, 1950-2, *Natural Religion and Christian Theology*, Vol. 1, p. 38.

No Longer Soloists

In so far as we allow ourselves to give ear to the solicitations—countless in number even if slight in substance—which come to us from the invisible world, then the whole outlook undergoes a change: and by that I mean that the transformation takes place *here below*, for earthly life itself is at the same time transfigured, it clothes itself in a dignity which cannot be allowed to it if it is looked at as some sort of excrescence which has budded erratically on a world which is in itself foreign to the spirit and to all its demands. Let me make use again of one of the musical comparisons for which you know I have a taste, and say that from the moment when we open ourselves to these infiltrations of the invisible, we cease to be the unskilled and yet pretentious soloists we perhaps were at the start, and gradually become members, wide-eyed and brotherly, of an orchestra in which those whom we so inaptly call the dead are quite certainly much closer to Him of whom we should not perhaps say that He conducts the symphony, but that He *is* the symphony in its profound and intelligible unity; a unity in which we can hope to be included only by degrees, through individual trials, the sum total of which, though it cannot be foreseen by each of us, is inseparable from his own vocation.

GABRIEL MARCEL, Aberdeen, 1949-50, *The Mystery of Being*, Vol. 2, p. 187.

Fulfilment in Religion

Psychologists today are insisting how absolutely fundamental in the human person is the need to be loved and to be aware that one is loved, and how useless it is to seek to heal and integrate the mind, or to give it strength to sustain the tasks and burdens of life, when that primordial need of the soul is not being satisfied. This cannot be without significance. Human love, however, is itself subject to all the imperfections and frustrations of man's life. It is only when the awareness of being loved is carried up into a man's relationship to the ultimate reality on whom all things and all values depend, that the self comes to rest in a sense of final fulfilment and wholeness which is not affected by the fact that all else in man's life is made—in the Apostle's words—'subject to vanity'. All other values are in principle secure in the eternal love of God which, claiming all and giving all, here and now (and not merely hereafter) sets man in the blessedness of fellowship with itself.

This is but to state in abstract terms what breaks forth in more than one place in the New Testament in words which are warm with conviction and feeling. 'Beloved, *now* are we the sons of God, and it doth not yet appear what we shall be.' 'All things are yours . . . whether the world, or life, or death, or things present, or things to come; all are yours; and ye are Christ's; and Christ is God's.' And most eloquent of all, is the passage in which the Apostle, having spoken with the utmost realism of the frustrations and sufferings of this present life and of the hope of the glory of the divine kingdom yet to be, nevertheless concludes that in all such frustrations and sufferings we are more than conquerors (*more* than conquerors because *merely* to conquer might mean no more than grimly and stoically to endure) through Him that *loved* us. 'For I am persuaded that neither death, nor life, nor angels, nor principalities, nor powers, nor things present, nor things to come, nor height, nor depth, nor any other creature, shall be able to separate us from the love of God, which is in Christ Jesus our Lord.'

HERBERT HENRY FARMER, Glasgow, 1949-50, *Revelation and Religion*, pp. 204-5.

154

From Death to Life

It is by living resolutely (as Goethe said) in the whole, the good, and the beautiful, that the Soul wins its eternal life. As we rise to this sphere, we apprehend more and more significant facts about existence. The lower facts are not lost or forgotten, but they fall into their true place, on a greatly reduced scale. Mere time-succession, as well as local position, becomes relatively unimportant. The date and duration of life are seen to be very insignificant facts. Individuality, as determined by local separation in different bodies, and not on distinctions of character, is seen to be a very small matter. On the other hand, the great unselfish interests, such as science and love of knowledge of all kinds, the love of art and beauty in all its forms, and above all goodness in its purest form—unselfish affection—are seen to be the true life of the Soul. In attaining this life it has in a sense to pass out of the normal soul-life into a higher sphere, not dominated by time: it has passed from death unto life, and enjoys eternal life though in the midst of time. Christ says quite explicitly that we can only save our Souls by losing them; that is to say, the Soul must sacrifice what seem at the time to be its own interests, in the service of the higher life which it will one day call its own. The Soul thus enters heaven by 'ascending in heart and mind' to 'the things that are above'—above itself.

The religious faith in immortality is the faith that all true values are valid always and everywhere; that the order of the universe is just, rational, and beautiful; and that those principles which exalt us above ourselves and open heaven to us are the attributes of the Creator in whom we live and move and have our being.

WILLIAM RALPH INGE, St Andrews, 1917-18, *The Philosophy of Plotinus*, Vol. 2, p. 28.

155

The Realization of Value

If absorption is not the goal, and free minds still endure, it is hardly possible to regard them as passing their time in the restful bliss of some paradise of the medieval pattern. For a life such as that—if life it can be called—would do little or nothing to bring to light the values and capacity for the creation of values which are the ripe fruit of moral experience. Beautiful souls are always something more than beautiful; they have a moral energy which inactivity would not content. Surely there has been much irrelevant suffering in the making of such souls if, after the struggle has given them command of circumstances, all enterprise is shut off from them.

What lies beyond we cannot tell, and it is vain to imagine. 'It doth not yet appear what we shall be.' But if free minds endure, it must surely be for a range of activity suited to the capacities and values which they have acquired in their mundane experience. And if, here or elsewhere, they attain that complete harmony between will and ideal in which moral perfection exists, they will surely be fitted thereby for nobler enterprises. . . . There would still be call and room for pressing further into the unknown and making all things subservient to the values which it is the function of free man to realize.

WILLIAM RITCHIE SORLEY, Aberdeen, 1914-15, *Moral Values and the Idea of God*, pp. 525-6.

156

Man no Fit Subject for Immortality?

Man, if we look at him as entirely absorbed in his finite activities, is no fit subject for immortality; there is no more call to raise the question in his case than in the case of other animals. This is the key to Hume's negative treatment of the subject in his unpublished essay on the Immortality of the Soul. . . . The reason is, as I have suggested, that Hume deliberately confined his survey to man's biological activities as a member of an animal species. Looking at him thus, he concludes that, 'if any purpose of nature be clear, we may affirm that the whole scope and intention of man's creation, so far as we can judge by natural reason, is limited to the present life. . . . If the reason of man gives him a great superiority over other animals, his necessities are proportionally multiplied upon him. His whole time, his whole capacity, activity, courage, passion, find sufficient employment in fencing against the miseries of his present condition, and frequently, nay almost always, are too slender for the business assigned them. . . . The powers of men are no more superior to their wants, considered merely in this life, than those of foxes and hares are, compared to *their* wants and to *their* period of existence. The inference from parity of reasoning is therefore obvious.'

Certainly, if reason were no more than this—a more effective weapon in the struggle for existence—Hume's argument would hold: man's life would be altogether on the same scale as that of foxes and hares, his outlook and activities limited, like theirs, to the present scene. There is nothing here to differentiate reason from instinct; one or two instincts thrown in might have served the purpose more effectively. But Hume deliberately ignores the fact that it is just by the operation of reason that the finite completeness of the merely animal life is broken up. . . . Art and science, morality and religion, all have their roots in reason, and these are to us the charter of our common humanity.

ANDREW SETH PRINGLE-PATTISON, Edinburgh, 1922, *The Idea of Immortality*, pp. 198-200.

157

Personal Survival

In brief, our plea for personal survival can be set out as follows. We have been led by the processes of reason to postulate that the world is the realm of Creative Spirit, of Mind which is purposive. Argument from the existence of the Moral Law or, in other words, of man's feeling that he is compelled to believe that goodness is objectively valid— such argument leads us to the conclusion that the Creative Spirit, in and for Whom the Universe exists, is good. But our arguments must be pronounced unsatisfactory, and the conclusions derived from them must be rejected, unless personal immortality be a fact.

Thus the witness of the moral consciousness and a conviction that the Universe is rational are the bases of our belief that human personality survives bodily death. It is not that we greedily demand another life to make amends for what we have suffered here. Probably most religious men ask nothing for themselves: their attitude is rather 'though He slay me, yet will I trust Him'. Yet it is our profound conviction that, to use words suggested by Henry Sidgwick (1838-1900), the good of the individual must be in some way identified with Universal Good. If no such identification is possible, the scheme of things, as we are compelled to regard it, is fundamentally irrational.

ERNEST WILLIAM BARNES, Aberdeen, 1927-9, *Scientific Theory and Religion*, pp. 645-6.

The Destiny of the Individual

The conclusion of our inquiry . . . into the bearing of a doctrine of Personality in God upon the problem of the destiny of the individual human person is that this doctrine, understood as we have understood it, as the theological expression of an experience of personal intercourse between the worshipper and the Object of his worship, affords the only truly positive ground of which a Gifford Lecturer can take cognizance for a belief in future blessedness and immortality, such as can form an article in a religious creed. It does not, as we have seen, enable us to meet directly the insistent doubts suggested by our experience of the constant association of personal spirit with a body forming part of the system studied by the natural sciences. Such difficulties might be, at least negatively, met by convincing evidence of the kind alleged by some votaries of what is called 'psychical research'. But this evidence, so far as it went, would remove the subject from the context of religious *faith.*

If, however, the supreme and central fact of the universe is a personal Love, it is intelligible that the apprehension of this fact and of its implications for created persons, should be inaccessible to those cognitive activities which do not involve a *personal* orientation such as is expressed by the word 'faith'.

We have to note, moreover, that, unless religious experience (and that not only in the form which expresses itself most naturally in the doctrine of Personality in God) is altogether an illusion, it cannot be explained on the principle of a pure Naturalism. Nor is it only religious experience of which this may be said. Science itself cannot be materialistically explained. . . . The man who takes Religion into account is better able than the materialist to be true to all sides of human experience. And out of the experience of Religion springs the hope of Immortality.

CLEMENT CHARLES JULIAN WEBB, Aberdeen, 1918-19, *Divine Personality and Human Life*, pp. 284-5.

XII

EARNEST ENQUIRERS
AFTER TRUTH

The lecturers appointed shall be subjected to no test of any kind, and shall not be required to take an oath, or to emit or subscribe any declaration of belief, or to make any promise of any kind; they may be of any denomination whatever, or of no denomination at all (and many earnest and high-minded men prefer to belong to no ecclesiastical denomination); they may be of any religion or way of thinking, or, as is sometimes said, they may be of no religion, or they may be so-called sceptics or agnostics or freethinkers, provided only that the 'patrons' will use diligence to secure that they be able reverent men, true thinkers, sincere lovers of and earnest enquirers after truth.

Earnest Enquiry

It was the object of Lord Gifford's bequest to untie the hands of combatants, but at the same time to fix the conditions on which the combat should be conducted. What was wanted for that purpose, as he declared in his will, were 'reverent men, true thinkers, sincere lovers, and earnest enquirers after truth'. These words are not used at random. Each sentence seems to have been carefully chosen and attentively weighed by him. He felt that religion was not a subject like other subjects, but that, whether on account of its age or owing to its momentous bearing on human welfare, it ought to be treated with due care and respect. *Reverence* alone, however, would not be sufficient, but should be joined with true thinking. *True thinking* means free thinking, thinking following its own laws, and unswayed by anything else. Think what thinking would be, if it were not free! But even this would not suffice. There ought to be not only loyal submission to the laws of thought, there ought to be a *sincere love*, a deep felt yearning for truth. And lastly, that love should not manifest itself in impatient and fanatical outbursts, but in *earnest enquiry*, in patient study, in long-continued research.

FRIEDRICH MAX MULLER, Glasgow, 1888-92, *Anthropological Religion*, pp. 16-17.

We Know in Part

A theology which finds mystery it cannot explain away at the centre of things may not be true, but it is certain that a theology which professes to have cleared away all the mystery out of the world must be false. In any account of the concrete and individual reality one must somewhere come upon something of which it can only be said, 'Why this thing should be so, or even just what it is, is more than I can tell, but at all costs it must be recognized that here the thing is. . . .'

So far as I can see, the function of authority is just to insist upon the reality and omnipresence in religion, as in all our contact with the objectively real, of this element of refractoriness to complete intellectual analysis which is the stamp of objectivity, this never wholly removable misfit between the real and the categories in which we try to confine it. 'A God comprehended is no God'; also, a 'nature' completely comprehended would not be the real natural world. But the misfit is so much more patent when it is God who is the object of our thinking, because of the incomparable wealth of intrinsic reality in the object. In dealing with a God who does not simply stand aloof 'on the other side', but has entered into the historical and become truly immanent in it, though never merely immanent, authority provides us with a way of escape from the agnosticism which is the despair of the intellect. . . . Or, to put it rather differently, what I would suggest is that authority and experience do not stand over against one another in sharp and irreconcilable opposition; authority is the self-assertion of the reality of an experience which contains more than any individual experient has succeeded in analysing out and extricating for himself. It is indispensable for us as finite historical beings who need a safeguard against our inveterate tendency to supplement the statement 'this is what I can make of this situation' by the perilous addition, 'and this is all there is in it'.

ALFRED EDWARD TAYLOR, St Andrews, 1926-7, *The Faith of a Moralist*, Vol. 2, pp. 212-14.

161

Poetry and Religion

If I read an account of a poem in a history of literature, I know something about it; but it is equally true that I do not thereby know the poem at all. I do that only in so far as it relives itself in me and becomes, in imagination, *my* expression. Hence it is possible for a man to know, in one sense, all the poetry that exists in the record of mankind and yet never, in a true sense, to have come into contact at all with the fact called poetry. So it is with religion. I may with sufficient labour know all that can be known about the outward facts of a given religion—its beliefs and acts and institutions; but all this is a mere *caput mortuum* unless I can in some measure relive in imagination the inner experience that formed the soul of this body.

Now to do this is, in many cases, possible only in the most meagre degree, and that is the reason why the study of religion is in some ways so disappointing. We know that such and such a people worshipped, as we say, such and such a god. But what this really means, what they felt in worshipping him, what made them regard him as adorable, what (as we say) went on inside them, how exactly, for example, a man imagined and felt when he bowed his whole soul before a thing in which we see next to nothing—this we cannot get at: and, if we cannot get at it at all, then I say we are no more in possession of the whole fact of that religion than a perfectly prosaic reader is in possession of a poem.

ANDREW CECIL BRADLEY, Glasgow, 1907, *Ideals of Religion*, pp. 11-12.

162

The Place of Minds in the World

The sensible world is the surface of nature; it consists of phenomena, and therefore answers all its own questions. The deep questions that seek a better grasp accept the surface, and their answers have to be verified by it. There is the same route for mind; the course of feeling, consciousness of every kind, is the mental surface; it is called the subject, being organized with reference to objects. That is also the concern which accounts for the coming of minds, and for their place in the world. The advance from physical to mental life advances nature from a world of stimuli as causes, to a world of objects as causes. Whether this world is nature proper is a question that soon includes the other worlds as well, in which we live and place ourselves. Nothing answers it but the objects themselves in their worlds. To make anything object is to make it declare itself.

Minds in living prove themselves, and . . . knowing is living and not only a means of living.

Reason makes things intelligible in the sense that the eye makes them visible, and the hand makes them hard. And though eye and ear grasp their object with ease, and need no learning, while understanding is laborious, the difference is one of degree. There is a complexity in music and design which it needs pains from ear and eye to comprehend. Sense comprehends one kind of object, understanding another, but they both comprehend, as well as apprehend. An object of sense is felt as one, though it is many, because the factors are felt in connexion with one another. We begin to understand both it and them, when we analyse it into them and their connexions.

WILLIAM MITCHELL, Aberdeen, 1924-6, *The Place of Minds in the World*, pp. viii, 6 and 106.

163

The Positivist Veto

According to this view a clear-headed modern philosopher should not try to erect cosmologies, to build theologies, to interpret theophanies, or even, like Marx, to construct a semi-economic philosophical fable. In the past (we are told) such attempts acquired an unearned increment of unwarranted prestige because of the presumed alliance between this kind of philosophy and the scientific part of philosophy. Nowadays (it is said) that support must be withdrawn and most that is called philosophy is only a species of poetry, a species moreover which, regarded as poetry, is not the best in that kind.

When Hume, like a second Caliph Omar, proposed that our libraries should be cleansed and also greatly lightened by committing to the flames all the volumes that did not deal either with formal mathematical demonstration or with experiments into matters-of-fact, it was the books about divinity and school metaphysics that he thought most deserving of combustion. The logical positivists of today say the same thing with all the emphasis at their command. Kant's 'critique of all theology' was not wholly dissimilar and Comte, as everyone knows, held that the metaphysical as well as the theological stage of speculation had to be outgrown before the human intellect attained its true majority in the understanding of positive science. Such a contemporary writer as Neurath follows Comte very closely indeed.

In opposition to these prevalent views, then, I am asserting that philosophy, philosophical theology and metaphysics, as I interpret these studies, are not a kind of poetry, and should not be confused with poetry. I do not say they are sciences in every sense of that hospitable term. They may not all be of the purest analytical water or meticulously experimental, but they are on the side of *scientia* in the general sense that they profess to be based upon reasoned argument, and, as I have said, to have their books ready for audit. How much is claimed for such enquiries is another story. 'I have never attempted to declare "the" truth' said Pherecydes in his 'letter' to Thales. 'I have simply said what a man may say who speaks of the gods. The rest is only conjecture.' That is still the spirit of natural theology. We are still asking whether a reasoned enquiry into the nature of things is evidence of the deiformity of reality. We still want to know whether we can only weave poetical myths about such matters, or can build on a solid foundation of rational argument.

JOHN LAIRD, Glasgow, 1939-40, *Theism and Cosmology*, pp. 32-3.

164

The Revolt against Reason

It is unnecessary, and would be out of place, to examine in detail the revolt against reason which has been so characteristic of recent orthodoxy. To ascribe it solely to the reaction against the identification of reason with scientific and quantitative studies would be to ignore two other elements which contribute to its support, the continuance of fundamentalist beliefs in the infallibility of Scripture and the revival of transcendentalist insistence upon the unknowable 'otherness' of God. Each of these characteristics found their prophet in Søren Kierkegaard, the Danish man of letters of a century ago; and the immense influence of his works during the past twenty years has been at once the sign and the instrument of irrationalism. They satisfied the longing for authority and pandered to the general despondency both by their denunciation of human thought and effort and by their insistence that the Word of God can only be accepted with creaturely and unquestioning obedience. They cut the sinews of faith by declaring that there could be no coming of God's Kingdom within history, and provided excuse for acquiescence in sin by proclaiming that fallen man could only face a choice of evils. To argue against them was impossible and wicked since reason was the enemy of faith and the proof of self-will.

Influential as this revolt has been, its error is evidenced not only by its character but by its effects. Reason may be, and is, a defective instrument: in its present obsession with the mathematical and quantitative it is obviously ill-fitted to deal with personal experience and the encounter of man with God. But although it is at best interpretative rather than creative, its function being to explain and so to enable communication, yet it is still our only means to this end, our sole instrument for the understanding and the debating of religion. Theology is only a handmaid of faith; but her service is indispensable. We can have, if we are worthy, good theology, if unworthy bad theology: an irrational theology would be a contradiction in terms; and a religion without theology would be a dumb and mutilated torso.

CHARLES EARLE RAVEN, Edinburgh, 1950-2, *Experience and Interpretation*, pp. 52-3.

165

Space-Time and Deity

In the religious emotion we have the direct experience of something higher than ourselves which we call God, which is not presented through the ways of sense but through this emotion. The emotion is our going out or endeavour or striving towards this object. Speculation enables us to say wherein the divine quality consists, and that it is an empirical quality the next in the series which the very nature of Time compels us to postulate, though we cannot tell what it is like. But besides assuring us of the place of the divine quality in the world, speculation has also to ask wherein this quality resides. What is the being which possesses deity? Our answer is to be a philosophical one; we are not concerned with the various forms which the conception of God has assumed in earlier or later religions. Ours is the modester

196

(and let me add far less arduous) inquiry what conception of God is required if we think of the universe as Space-Time engendering within itself in the course of time the series of empirical qualities of which deity is the one next ahead of mind. God is the whole world as possessing the quality of deity. Of such a being the whole world is the 'body' and deity is the 'mind'. But the possessor of deity is not actual but ideal. As an actual existent, God is the infinite world with its nisus towards deity, or, to adapt a phrase of Leibniz, as big or in travail with deity.

Since Space-Time is already a whole and one, why, it may be urged, should we seek to go beyond it? Why not identify God with Space-Time? Now, no one could worship Space-Time. It may excite speculative or mathematical enthusiasm and fill our minds with intellectual admiration, but it lights no spark of religious emotion. Worship is not the response which Space-Time evokes in us, but intuition. Even Kant's starry heavens are material systems, and he added the moral law to them in describing the source of our reverence. In one way this consideration is irrelevant; for if philosophy were forced to this conclusion that God is nothing but Space-Time, we should needs be content. But a philosophy which left one portion of human experience suspended without attachment to the world of truth is gravely open to suspicion; and its failure to make the religious emotion speculatively intelligible betrays a speculative weakness. For the religious emotion is one part of experience, and an empirical philosophy must include in one form or another the whole of experience.

SAMUEL ALEXANDER, Glasgow, 1916-18, *Space, Time and Deity*, pp. 352-3.

166

Emergent Evolution and God

I have, perhaps, given some evidence that I am not seriously deficient in natural piety. But go on my way rejoicing in the agnostic position I cannot. Presumably for better or worse I am that way constituted. At all events a supplementary concept of Activity seems to me, being what I am, called for. I frankly admit that I accept Activity under what I have called acknowledgment. This means that it lies beyond the range

197

of such positive proof as naturalistic criticism rightly demands. But I ask: Does it entail aught that is contradictory to the positive evidence? In any case I am prepared to face the risk. For me the acknowledgment takes the form of belief in God. But here I am content to lay the main stress on the concept of Activity. . . . Acknowledged Activity is *omnipresent throughout* if it be present at all. It will also, I suppose, be clear that the avenue of approach towards Activity in each one of us must be sought in some kind of immediate acquaintance within the current changes of one's own psychical system. All other avenues of approach must be indirect as the outcome of reference. Within us, if anywhere, we must feel the urge, or however it be named, which shall afford the basis upon which acknowledgment of Activity is founded. What then does it feel like? Each must answer for himself, fully realizing that he may misinterpret the evidence. Without denying a felt push from the lower levels of one's being—a so-called driving force welling up from below—to me it feels like a drawing upwards through Activity existent at a higher level than that to which I have attained. Of course, I am quite ready to admit that those who do have this feeling of being attracted by the Ideal and who build an explanation thereon, may be mistaken. Hence my reiterated speaking of acknowledgment. What I here acknowledge is a really existent Ideal, independent of my emergent ideals, and of the emergent quality of deity, in much the same sense as I acknowledge a physical world existent independently of my perceiving it.

CONWY LLOYD MORGAN, St Andrews, 1922-3, *Emergent Evolution*, pp. 207-9.

167

The Faith of a Scientist

In the official creeds and other formularies of existing Churches supernatural events are still a prominent feature. There are even influential sections within, at any rate, the English Church who wish to see, not less, but more of supernatural belief definitely countenanced. On the other hand, a very large and increasing body of persons who have studied or been influenced by one branch or another of science find themselves

198

unable to belong to any recognized Church, because they cannot accept any form of belief in what is supernatural. It is to this body that I myself belong, and, as you must have already seen, I am not here to support what seems to me unsatisfactory theology, but to carry out to the best of my ability the intention of the founder of the Gifford Lectureships. I can put my heart into this attempt because no one can feel more strongly than I do that religion is the greatest thing in life, and that behind the recognized Churches there is an unrecognized Church to which all may belong, though supernatural events play no part in its creed.

Belief in supernatural events is just the complement of the materialism associated with theology, though not with religion itself. If once we admit, as theologians have done, that the visible world is actually a material world, then supernatural events of various sorts have to be called in to justify religious belief. Supernatural creation, supernatural revelation, supernatural raising from the dead, and even supernatural action of the soul on the body, all become necessary. My own wish to see belief in the supernatural dissociated entirely from religion is only part of a wish to see materialism dissociated from it. The materialism with which orthodox theology is at present shot through and through is the whole source of the weakness of religious belief in presence of the sciences, and of the alienation between religious belief and the sciences. It ought to be added, however, that men of science themselves are equally to blame in this respect. They have, on the whole, disregarded philosophy completely. . . . They are in a similar position to that of the Schoolmen who despised experimental science.

JOHN SCOTT HALDANE, Glasgow, 1927-8, *The Sciences and Philosophy*, pp. 310-12.

Reality, Mathematics and Language

When we represent a group of connections by a closed and coherent set of concepts, axioms, definitions and laws which in turn is represented by a mathematical scheme we have in fact isolated and idealized this group of connections with the purpose of clarification. But even if complete clarity has been achieved in this way, it is not known how accurately the set of concepts described reality.

These idealizations may be called a part of the human language that has been formed from the interplay between the world and ourselves, a human response to the challenge of nature. In this respect they may be compared to the different styles of art, say of architecture or music. A style of art can also be defined by a set of formal rules which are applied to the material of this special art. These rules can perhaps not be represented in a strict sense by a set of mathematical concepts and equations, but their fundamental elements are very closely related to the essential elements of mathematics. Equality and inequality, repetition and symmetry, certain group structures play the fundamental role both in art and in mathematics. Usually the work of several generations is needed to develop that formal beginning to the wealth of elaborate forms which characterize its completion. The interest of the artist is concentrated on this system which later is called the style of the art, from its simple process of crystallization, where the material of the art takes, through his action, the various forms that are initiated by the first formal concepts of this style. After the completion the interest must face again, because the word 'interest' means: to be with something, to take part in a process of life, but this process has then come to an end. Here again the question of how far the formal rules of the style represent that reality of life which is meant by the art cannot be decided from the formal rules. Art is always an idealization; the ideal is different from the reality—at least from the reality of the shadows, as Plato would have put it—but idealization is necessary for understanding.

WERNER HEISENBERG, St Andrews, 1955-6, *Physics and Philosophy*, pp. 96-7.

169

Heuristic Commitment

The science of today serves as a heuristic guide for its own further development. It conveys a conception about the nature of things which suggest to the enquiring mind an inexhaustible range of surmises. The experience of Columbus, who so fatefully misjudged his own discovery, is inherent to some extent in all discovery. The implications of new knowledge can never be known at its birth. For it speaks of something real, and to attribute reality to something is to express the belief that its presence will yet show up in an indefinite number of unpredictable ways.

An empirical statement is true to the extent to which it reveals an aspect of reality, a reality largely hidden to us and *existing therefore independently of our knowing it*. By trying to say something that is true about a reality believed to be existing independently of our knowing it, all assertions of fact necessarily carry *universal intent*. *Our claim to speak of reality serves thus as the external anchoring of our commitment in making a factual statement.*

The framework of commitment is now established in outline for this particular case. The enquiring scientist's intimations of a hidden reality are personal. They are his own beliefs, which—owing to his originality—as yet he alone holds. Yet they are not a subjective state of mind, but convictions held with universal intent, and heavy with arduous projects. It was he who decided what to believe, yet there is no arbitrariness in his decision. For he arrived at his conclusions by the utmost exercise of responsibility. He has reached responsible beliefs, born of necessity, and not changeable at will. In a heuristic commitment, affirmation, surrender and legislation are fused into a single thought, bearing on a hidden reality.

To accept commitment as the only relation in which we can believe something to be true, is to abandon all efforts to find strict criteria of truth and strict procedures for arriving at the truth. A result obtained by applying strict rules mechanically, without committing anyone personally, can mean nothing to anybody.

MICHAEL POLANYI, Aberdeen, 1951-2, *Personal Knowledge*, p. 311.

170

The Crisis of the Personal

Existentialism has discovered, with sensitiveness of feeling, that the philosophical problem of the present lies in a crisis of the personal: logical empiricism recognizes it as a crisis of logical form and method.

Both are correct, and both are one-sided. The cultural crisis of the present is indeed a crisis of the personal. But the problem it presents to philosophy is a formal one. It is to discover or to construct the intellectual form of the personal.

. . . Since philosophy must include the personal in its field of inquiry, this can only mean that we must abandon the organic form as inadequate for the philosophical purpose, and initiate a search for the form of the personal.

If we are correct in suggesting that there is, in the modern period, a close relation between the development of science and of philosophy, this is the conclusion which we shall naturally expect. If science moves from established physics to the foundation of scientific biology, we find that philosophy moves from a mathematical to an organic form. We should expect, then, that the emergence of scientific psychology would be paralleled by a transition from an organic to a personal philosophy. The form of the personal will be the emergent problem. Such a new phase of philosophy would rest on the assertion that the self is neither a substance nor an organism, but a person. Its immediate task would be to discover the logical form through which the unity of the personal can be coherently conceived.

JOHN MACMURRAY, Glasgow, 1953-4, *The Self as Agent*, pp. 29, 37.

171

No Action without an Agent

A personal conception alone is fully theistic and fully religious. For there can be no action without an agent, and an agent, whether finite or infinite, though he is immanent in existence, necessarily transcends it. For the existent is what has been determined, and the agent is the determiner. What has been determined is the past; but the agent is concerned with the future and its determination. So in action he passes beyond his existence, transcending the past which constitutes his determinate being. His reality as agent lies in his continual self-transcendence. God, therefore, as the infinite Agent is immanent in the world which is his act, but transcendent of it. The terms 'transcendent' and 'immanent' refer to the nature of persons as agents, and they are strictly correlative. Pure immanence, like pure transcendence, is meaningless. Whatever is transcendent is necessarily immanent; and immanence, in turn, implies transcendence.

It would be a mistake to suppose that this vindication of the validity of religious belief in general constitutes an argument for the truth of any system of religious belief in particular. Religious doctrines are as problematic as scientific theories and require like them a constant revision and a continual verification in action. Their verification differs in this, that it cannot be experimental, since they are not merely pragmatic; they can be verified only by persons who are prepared to commit themselves intentionally to the way of life which they prescribe.

By shifting our standpoint from the 'I think' to the 'I do', we have restored the reference of thought to action, and in the result have found that we are driven to conceive a personal universe in which God is the ultimate reality. This transformation restores its whole substance to philosophy, which again becomes the intellectual aspect of the search for the real. The problematic of philosophy lies then in the distinction between 'real' and 'unreal'. Now this, as we have seen, is the problematic of religious reflection; and philosophy, if it is concerned with the intellectual aspect of this problematic, must be identical with theology, with an undogmatic theology, which, like science, has abandoned certainty, and which has recognized that religious doctrines, too, are all hypothetical. Philosophy, we must conclude, is theology which has abandoned dogmatism, and has become in a new and wider sense a Natural Theology.

JOHN MACMURRAY, Glasgow, 1953-4, *Persons in Relation*, pp. 223-4.

172

God-truth and World-truths

If it is true that the word of God is the truth, we have first to distinguish between Truth in the singular—which means God—and truths in the plural—which are truths about the world. As God is the Creator (and as such the primary reality) and the world His creation (and as such derived, conditioned and relative reality, having its ground in God), so there are also two kinds of truths: God-truth and world-truths. It is one of the great tragedies of Christian history that this distinction has not been carried through. Medieval theology—and with regard to this question Protestant orthodoxy takes the same view—considered the source of God-truth, revelation, Holy Scripture, as being also the truth and norm of world-knowledge. By so doing it has fettered the legitimate, scientific use of reason and stamped the world-picture of Biblical antiquity with the authority of divine revelation. Thus Copernicus had to be called a fool, and his successor Galileo, accused of heresy, because their teaching about the structure of the astronomical world was irreconcilable with the Biblical picture. For the same reason Darwin had to be called an enemy of God because he placed man as a 'zoon' within the great connection of the animal world. The Church conducted a miserable crusade against the young, serious and high-spirited scientific generation seeking truth—world-truth—at all cost.

Retribution was bound to come. Science paid the Church back, so to speak, in the same coin: in its turn it failed to distinguish between God-truth and world-truths. More and more, science claimed the monopoly of truth-knowledge. The positivistic view that only scientific knowledge has a legitimate claim to truth, and that nothing which is incapable of scientific proof can be true—this orthodoxy of scientific positivism, forming an exact parallel with medieval clerical orthodoxy—not merely has its following among philosophers and scientists, but has become a very popular and widespread creed.

EMIL BRUNNER, St Andrews, 1947-8, *Christianity and Civilisation*, Vol. I, pp. 35-6.

173

Optimism, Pessimism and Meliorism

'Optimism' and 'pessimism' are the names given to attitudes of hopefulness or hopelessness regarding the future—hoping the best, fearing the worst. . . .

An enlightened and candid reading of nature and history warrants neither a complete optimism nor a complete pessimism. There is a third possibility which is neither the one nor the other, nor a mere mixture or alternation of the two. This third possibility, which is closest to the attitude of common sense, combines acknowledgment of past and present evil with a hopeful resolve to achieve a better future. The name of this third religious attitude is 'meliorism'. . . .

Meliorism is not an 'easy' optimism, as the pessimist charges. It does not change its allegiance in order to be on the winning side. It does not fortify itself in an ivory tower; choosing only aesthetic or cognitive goods because they are safe, and abandoning the moral and social goods because they are exposed to mortal vicissitudes. It gives hostages to fortune, and determines to retrieve them.

A religion of meliorism is not guilty of ignoring or underrating evil; or of failing to see how ineradicable it is. Quite the contrary. All triumphs of the will are attended by the risk of failure, as all cognitive judgments are attended by the risk of error. There is no infallibility in either sphere. Man's fallibility does not demean him, but raises him to the level of a seeker for truth and a pursuer of good. Indeed, a divine being who could not fail or err would cease to be a voluntary or cognitive being.

Meliorism, then, does not choose the easy way: indeed, it denies that there is an easy way—any short cut, or detour, or patent remedy; and it *chooses* the hard way. It cherishes no illusions of a hollow or predetermined victory. It is aware of the possibility of failure. It accepts every evidence of the indifference of nature, of the baseness of human nature, and of the corruption of society. It chooses the hard way with its eyes open. It takes the bad news with the good; but it does not on that account surrender or leave the field of action. It summons courage to overcome discouragement.

RALPH BARTON PERRY, Glasgow, 1946-8, *Realms of Value*, pp. 486-8.

174

The Human Predicament

The distinction has been made between atheistic and theistic existentialism. Certainly there are existentialists who could be called 'atheistic', at least according to their intention; and there are others who can be called 'theistic'. But, in reality, there is no atheistic or theistic existentialism. Existentialism gives an analysis of what it means to exist. It shows the contrast between an essentialist description and an existentialist analysis. It develops the question implied in existence, but it does not try to give the answer, either in atheistic or in theistic terms. Whenever existentialists give answers, they do so in terms of religious or quasi-religious traditions which are not derived from their existential analysis. Pascal derives his answers from the Augustinian tradition, Kierkegaard from the Lutheran, Marcel from the Thomist, Dostoevski from the Greek Orthodox. Or the answers are derived from humanistic traditions, as with Marx, Sartre, Nietzsche, Heidegger, and Jaspers. None of these men was able to develop answers out of his questions. The answers of the humanists come from hidden religious sources. They are matters of ultimate concern or faith, although garbed in a secular gown. Hence the distinction between atheistic and theistic existentialism fails. Existentialism is an analysis of the human predicament. And the answers to the question implied in man's predicament are religious, whether open or hidden.

PAUL TILLICH, Aberdeen, 1953-4, *Systematic Theology*, Vol. 2, p. 28.

175

Irrational Dogmatism—No Foundation

Dogmatic theology may appear to those who have not the scientific outlook to be the only support now available for a religious faith that they 'feel in their bones' to be true. But a religion supported by such dogmatism can no longer appeal to the scientifically-minded modern man. The majority of intellectuals today tend to regard the western world as having passed into the post-Christian era and no longer regard themselves technically as Christians. Professor Leuba's questionnaire survey of the beliefs of eminent scholars in America in 1921 (omitting, of course, theologians and ministers of religion) gave the historians at the top of the list of those who believed in God, but among them only

48 per cent of them believed; the biologists and psychologists came at the bottom of their list with 31 and 24 per cent belief respectively. If such a survey were taken again today I expect that the figures would be much lower. I also believe, however, that few would deny that the Christian environment has been essential for the development of all that Western civilization stands for, including intellectual freedom. There is a danger of losing this if we lose the Christian spirit; and the danger of losing that spirit is greater if current theology tends to be tied to an irrational dogmatism.

For me it is this spirit of Christianity, not any hypothetical dogma of theology, that matters. Evidence of the working of a Divine Power that we may call God, the reality of religious experience, the sense of the sacred, and a belief in the way of life as taught in the Gospel of Jesus—a belief men have died for—these, to my mind, are vital; for me they form a far more substantial foundation for a theology than the blind acceptance of supposed events in the past—events which cannot satisfy the accepted rules of evidence used in other fields of historical research.

ALISTER HARDY, Aberdeen 1963-5, *The Divine Flame*, pp. 212-13.

176

The Eschatological Moment

The meaning in history lies always in the present, and when the present is conceived as the eschatological present by Christian faith the meaning in history is realized. Man who complains: 'I cannot see meaning in history, and therefore my life, interwoven in history, is meaningless', is to be admonished: do not look around yourself into universal history, you must look into your own personal history. Always in your present lies the meaning in history, and you cannot see it as a spectator, but only in your responsible decisions. In every moment slumbers the possibility of being the eschatological moment. You must awaken it.

RUDOLF BULTMANN, Edinburgh, 1954-5, *History and Eschatology*, p. 155.

The Last Word with Plato

The question of religion, like that of morality, is not one of theory: it is a question of the life a man is going to lead. This is a matter for personal decision and personal commitment in a world in which we can know only the surface appearance, although there is no need to surround this with portentousness and despair. For the religious man the decision may come only by the grace of God, but even so it should not be taken blindly in the dark. The leap of faith—or the leap of doubt—should be made in the light of all that each man can know, not merely of science, but of action and of art and of religion itself.

The predicament caused by the gulf between faith and knowledge is acute in the modern world, but it is also very old. Perhaps I cannot do better than conclude with some words which in the *Phaedo* Plato puts into the mouth of Simmias:

'I think, Socrates, as perhaps you do yourself, that about such matters it is either impossible or supremely difficult to acquire clear knowledge in our present life. Yet it is cowardly not to test in every way what we are told about them, or to give up before we are worn out with studying them from every point of view. For we ought to do one of the following things: either we should learn the truth about them from others; or we should find it out for ourselves; or, if this is impossible, we should take what is at least the best human account of them, the one hardest to disprove, and sailing on it, as on a raft, we should voyage through life in the face of risks—unless one might be able on some stouter vessel, some divine account, to make the journey with more assurance and with fewer perils.'

HERBERT JAMES PATON, St Andrews, 1949-50, *The Modern Predicament*, p. 388.

APPENDIX I

Gifford Lecturers and Bibliography of Published Gifford Lectures
(Extract numbers are shown in square brackets)

ADAM, JAMES (1860-1907), Aberdeen, 1904-06, Fellow and Senior Tutor
of Emmanuel College, Cambridge, *The Religious Teachers of Greece*,
Edinburgh, 1908 [25]

ALEXANDER, SAMUEL (1859-1938), Glasgow, 1916-18, Professor of Philosophy, University of Manchester, *Space Time and Deity*, 1920, two
volumes [165]

BAILLIE, JOHN (1886-1960), Edinburgh, 1961-2,[1] Professor of Divinity
and Principal of New College, Edinburgh, *The Sense of the Presence of
God*, 1962 [39, 44, 116]

BALFOUR, ARTHUR JAMES (1848-1930), Glasgow, 1914 and 1922-3,
Member of Parliament, *Theism and Humanism*, 1915 [17], *Theism and
Thought*, 1923 [13]

BARNES, ERNEST WILLIAM (1874-1953), Aberdeen, 1927-9, Bishop of
Birmingham, *Scientific Theory and Religion*, Cambridge, 1933 [65, 108,
157]

BARTH, KARL (1886-1969), Aberdeen, 1937-8, Professor of Theology,
University of Basle, *The Knowledge of God and the Service of God*, 1938
[10, 45]

BEVAN, EDWYN ROBERT (1870-1943), Edinburgh, 1933-4, Lecturer in
Hellenistic History and Literature, King's College, London, *Symbolism
and Belief*, 1938, *Holy Images*, 1940 [46, 50, 90]

BIDEZ, JOSEPH (1867-1945), St Andrews, 1938-9, Professor of Classical
Philology and the History of Philosophy, University of Ghent, *Eos* ou
Platon et l'Orient, Bruxelles, 1945

BLANSHARD, BRAND (1892-   ), St Andrews, 1951-3, Professor of
Philosophy, Yale University, *Reason and Goodness*, 1961 [135]

BOSANQUET, BERNARD (1848-1923), Edinburgh, 1911-12, Professor of
Moral Philosophy, University of St Andrews, *The Principle of Individuality and Value*, 1912 [85], *The Value and Destiny of the Individual*,
1913 [61]

BOUTROUX, EMILE (1845-1921), Glasgow, 1903-05, Professor of Philosophy, University of Paris, *Science and Religion in Contemporary
Philosophy*,[2] trans. J. Nield, 1909 [104]

BRADLEY, ANDREW CECIL (1851-1935), Glasgow, 1907-08, Professor of
Poetry, University of Oxford, *Ideals of Religion*, 1940 [143, 161]

BRUCE, ALEXANDER BALMAIN (1831-1899), Glasgow, 1897-8, Professor of

---

[1] The lectures were not delivered but were accorded the status of Gifford
Lectures posthumously.
[2] This volume is not acknowledged as being the Gifford Lectures but appears
to contain much of the material used.

Exegesis, Free Church College, Glasgow, *The Providential Order of the World*, 1897 [81, 125], *The Moral Order of the World*, 1899 [30]

BRUNNER, EMIL (1889-1966), St Andrews, 1947, Professor of Systematic and Practical Theology, University of Zürich, *Christianity and Civilisation*, two volumes, 1948, 1949 [67, 142, 172]

BULTMANN, RUDOLF KARL (1884-   ), Edinburgh, 1954-5, Professor of New Testament Studies, Marburg, *History and Eschatology*, Edinburgh, 1958 [93, 176]

CAIRD, EDWARD (1835-1908), St Andrews, 1890-2, Professor of Moral Philosophy, University of Glasgow, *The Evolution of Religion*, two volumes, Glasgow, 1894 [43]. Glasgow, 1900-02. Master of Balliol College, Oxford, *The Evolution of Theology in the Greek Philosophers*, two volumes, Glasgow, 1904 [11, 31]

CAIRD, JOHN (1820-1898), Glasgow, 1892-3 and 1895-6, Principal of the University of Glasgow, *The Fundamental Ideas of Christianity*, two volumes, Glasgow, 1899 [54, 117]

CAMPBELL, CHARLES ARTHUR (1897-   ), St Andrews, 1953-5, Professor of Logic and Rhetoric, University of Glasgow, *On Selfhood and Godhood*, 1957 [4, 49]

CAMPBELL, LEWIS (1830-1908), St Andrews, 1894-6, Emeritus Professor of Greek, University of St Andrews, *Religion in Greek Literature*, 1898 [150]

DAWSON, CHRISTOPHER (1889-1970), Edinburgh, 1947-9, *Religion and Culture*, 1948 [38], *Religion and the Rise of Western Culture*, 1950 [34]

DE BURGH, WILLIAM GEORGE (1866-1943), St Andrews, 1937-8, Emeritus Professor of Philosophy, University of Reading, *From Morality to Religion*, 1938 [64, 144]

DEWEY, JOHN (1899-1952), Edinburgh, 1928-9, Professor of Philosophy, Columbia University, *The Quest for Certainty*, 1930 [130, 138]

DIXON, WILLIAM MCNEILE (1866-1946), Glasgow, 1935-7, Emeritus Professor of English Language and Literature, University of Glasgow, *The Human Situation*, 1937 [111]

DRIESCH, HANS (1867-1941), Aberdeen, 1907-08, Professor of Philosophy, University of Heidelberg, *Science and Philosophy of Organism*, two volumes, 1908 [105]

EDDINGTON, ARTHUR STANLEY (1882-1944), Edinburgh, 1927, Plumian Professor of Astronomy, University of Cambridge, *The Nature of the Physical World*, Cambridge, 1928 [102, 103]

FAIRBAIRN, ANDREW MARTIN (1838-1912), Aberdeen, 1891-3, Principal of Mansfield College, Oxford, *The Philosophy of the Christian Religion*,[1] 1902 [58]

FARMER, HERBERT HENRY (1892-   ), Glasgow, 1949-50, Professor of Systematic Theology and Apologetics, Westminster College, Cambridge, *Revelation and Religion*, 1954 [19, 153]

---

[1] This volume is not acknowledged as being the Gifford Lectures but appears to contain much of the material used.

FARNELL, LEWIS RICHARD (1856-1934), St Andrews, 1919-20 and 1924-5, Rector of Exeter College, Oxford, *Greek Hero Cults*, 1921 [145], *The Attributes of God*, 1925 [48, 70]

FARRER, AUSTIN MARSDEN (1904-1969), Edinburgh, 1956-7, Fellow and Chaplain, Trinity College, Oxford, *The Freedom of the Will*, 1958 [131]

FINDLAY, JOHN NIEMAYER (1903-   ), St Andrews, 1964-6, Professor of Philosophy, King's College, University of London, *The Discipline of the Cave*, 1966, *The Transcendence of the Cave*, 1967 [69]

FOWLER, WILLIAM WARDE (1847-1921), Edinburgh, 1909-10, Tutor and Fellow of Lincoln College, University of Oxford, *The Religious Experience of the Roman People*, 1911 [29]

FRASER, ALEXANDER CAMPBELL (1819-1914), Edinburgh, 1894-6, Professor of Logic and Metaphysics, University of Edinburgh, *The Philosophy of Theism*, two volumes, 1894 [98, 125]

FRAZER, JAMES GEORGE (1854-1941), St Andrews, 1911-13, Professor of Social Anthropology, University of Liverpool, *The Belief in Immortality*, 1913, Edinburgh, 1924-5 [148], *The Worship of Nature*, 1926 [22, 23]

GILSON, ETIENNE (1884-   ), Aberdeen, 1931-2, Professor of Medieval Philosophy, Sorbonne, *The Spirit of Mediaeval Philosophy*, trans. A. H. C. Downes, 1936 [12, 35, 99]

GORE, CHARLES (1853-1932), St Andrews, 1929-30, Sometime Bishop of Oxford, *The Philosophy of the Good Life*, 1930 [77]

GWATKIN, HENRY MELVILL (1844-1916), Edinburgh, 1903-05, Dixie Professor of Ecclesiastical History, Cambridge, *The Knowledge of God*, two volumes, Edinburgh, 1906 [28, 86]

HALDANE, JOHN SCOTT (1860-1936), Glasgow, 1927-8, Fellow of New College, Oxford, *The Sciences and Philosophy*, 1929 [126, 167]

HALDANE, RICHARD BURDON (1856-1928), St Andrews, 1902-04, Viscount Haldane of Cloan, *The Pathway to Reality*, two volumes, 1903 and 1904 [41, 52]

HARDY, ALISTER (1896-   ), Aberdeen, 1963-5, Emeritus Professor of Zoology, University of Oxford, *The Living Stream*, 1965 [112], *The Divine Flame*, 1966 [20, 175]

HEISENBERG, WERNER CARL (1901-   ), St Andrews, 1955-6, Director of Max Planck Institute of Physics, Göttingen, *Physics and Philosophy*, 1959 [106, 168]

HENSON, HERBERT HENSLEY (1863-1947), St Andrews, 1935-6, Bishop of Durham, *Christian Morality, Natural, Developing, Final*, Oxford, 1936 [33, 141]

HOBSON, ERNEST WILLIAM (1850-1933), Aberdeen, 1921-2, Sadleirian Professor of Pure Mathematics, University of Cambridge, *The Domain of Natural Science*, Cambridge, 1923 [76, 122]

HODGSON, LEONARD (1889-1969), Glasgow, 1955-7, Regius Professor of Divinity, University of Oxford, *For Faith and Freedom*, two volumes, Oxford, 1956 and 1957 [95, 119]

INGE, WILLIAM RALPH (1860-1954), St Andrews, 1917-18, Dean of St

Paul's Cathedral, London, *The Philosophy of Plotinus*, two volumes, 1918 [68, 154]

JAEGER, WERNER (1889-1961), St Andrews, 1936, Professor of Classical Literature, University of California, *The Theology of the Early Greek Philosophers*, Oxford, 1947 [8]

JAMES, WILLIAM (1842-1910), Edinburgh, 1901-02, Professor of Philosophy, Harvard University, *The Varieties of Religious Experience*, 1902 [59, 66, 88]

JONES, HENRY (1852-1922), Glasgow, 1920-1, Professor of Moral Philosophy, University of Glasgow, *A Faith that Enquires*, 1922 [57, 73]

KNOX, MALCOLM (1900-   ), Aberdeen, 1966-8, Professor of Moral Philosophy, University of St Andrews, *Action*, 1968 [134], *A Layman's Quest*, 1969

KRONER, RICHARD (1884-   ), St Andrews, 1939-40, Sometime Professor of Philosophy, University of Kiel, *The Primacy of Faith*, New York, 1943 [62, 63]

LAIRD, JOHN (1887-1946), Glasgow, 1939-40, Professor of Moral Philosophy, University of Aberdeen, *Theism and Cosmology*, 1940 [163], *Mind and Deity*, 1941 [18]

LANCIANI, RODOLFO AMEDEO (1846-1929), St Andrews, 1899-1901, Professor of Ancient Topography, University of Rome, *New Tales of Old Rome*, 1901 [32]

LANG, ANDREW (1844-1912), St Andrews, 1888-90, Sometime Fellow of Merton College, University of Oxford, *The Making of Religion*, 1898 [21, 146]

LAURIE, SIMON SOMERVILLE (1829-1909), Edinburgh, 1905-06, Professor of Education, University of Edinburgh, *Synthetica*, Volume 2, 1906 [79]

MACBEATH, ALEXANDER MURRAY (1888-   ), St Andrews, 1948-9, Professor of Logic and Metaphysics, Queen's University, Belfast, *Experiments in Living*, 1952 [140]

MACMURRAY, JOHN (1891-   ), Glasgow, 1953-4, Professor of Moral Philosophy, University of Edinburgh, *The Self as Agent*, 1957 [127, 170], *Persons in Relation*, 1961 [171]

MARCEL, GABRIEL (1889-   ), Aberdeen, 1949-50, French Writer and Philosopher, *The Mystery of Being—1. Reflection and Mystery*, trans. G. S. Fraser, 1950 [78], *The Mystery of Being—2. Faith and Reality*, trans. Rene Hague, 1951 [94, 152]

MARETT, ROBERT RANULPH (1866-1943), St Andrews, 1931-2, Rector of Exeter College, Oxford, *Faith, Hope and Charity in Primitive Religion*, Oxford, 1932 [24], *Sacraments of Simple Folk*, Oxford, 1933 [147]

MITCHELL, WILLIAM (1861-1962), Aberdeen, 1924-6, Professor of Philosophy, University of Adelaide, Australia, *The Place of Minds in the World*, 1933 [162]

MORGAN, CONWY LLOYD (1852-1936), St Andrews, 1922-3, Emeritus Professor of Zoology and Geology, University of Bristol, *Emergent Evolution*, 1923 [166], *Life, Mind and Spirit*, 1926 [123]

MÜLLER, FRIEDRICH MAX (1823-1900), Glasgow, 1888-92, Professor of

Comparative Philology, University of Oxford, *Natural Religion*, 1889 [1, 7], *Physical Religion*, 1891, *Anthropological Religion*, 1892 [159], *Theosophy or Psychological Religion*, 1893

NIEBUHR, REINHOLD (1892-   ), Edinburgh, 1939, Professor of Ethics and Theology, Union Theological Seminary, New York, *The Nature and Destiny of Man*, two volumes, 1941 and 1943 [36, 71]

PATERSON, WILLIAM PATERSON (1860-1939), Glasgow, 1924-5, Professor of Divinity, University of Edinburgh, *The Nature of Religion*, 1925 [89]

PATON, HERBERT JAMES (1887-1969), St Andrews, 1949-50, White's Professor of Moral Philosophy, University of Oxford, *The Modern Predicament*, 1955 [3, 9, 84, 177]

PERRY, RALPH BARTON (1876-1957), Glasgow, 1947-8, Professor of Philosophy, Harvard University, *Realms of Value*, Cambridge, Mass., 1954 [60, 139, 173]

PFLEIDERER, OTTO (1839-1908), Edinburgh, 1892-4, Professor of Theology, University of Berlin, *Philosophy and Development of Religion*, two volumes, 1894 [16, 37]

POLANYI, MICHAEL (1891-   ), Aberdeen, 1951-2, Professor of Social Studies, University of Manchester, *Personal Knowledge*, 1958 [124, 169]

PRICE, HENRY HABBERLEY (1899-   ), Aberdeen, 1959-61, Wykeham Professor of Logic and Fellow of New College, Oxford, *Belief*, 1969 [40]

PRINGLE-PATTISON, ANDREW SETH (1856-1931), Aberdeen, 1912-13, Professor of Logic and Metaphysics, University of Edinburgh, *The Idea of God in the Light of Recent Philosophy*, Oxford, 1920 [47], Edinburgh, 1922-3, Emeritus Professor, University of Edinburgh, *The Idea of Immortality*, Oxford, 1922 [156], *Studies in the Philosophy of Religion*, Oxford, 1930 [129]

RAMSAY, WILLIAM MITCHELL (1851-1939), Edinburgh, 1915-16, Sometime Regius Professor of Humanity, Aberdeen, *Asianic Elements in Greek Civilisation*, 1927 [83]

RAVEN, CHARLES EARLE (1885-1964), Edinburgh, 1950-2, Regius Professor Emeritus of Divinity, University of Cambridge, *Natural Religion and Christian Theology*, two volumes, Cambridge, 1953 [151, 164]

ROSS, WILLIAM DAVID (1877-   ), Aberdeen, 1935-6, Provost of Oriel College, Oxford, *Foundations of Ethics*, Oxford, 1939 [132, 133]

ROYCE, JOSIAH (1855-1916), Aberdeen, 1899-1900, Professor of the History of Philosophy, Harvard University, *The World and the Individual*, two volumes, New York, 1900 and 1901 [42]

RUNCIMAN, STEVEN (1903-   ), St Andrews, 1960-2, Fellow of Trinity College, Cambridge, *The Great Church in Captivity*, Cambridge, 1968

SAYCE, ARCHIBALD HENRY (1845-1933), Aberdeen, 1900-02, Professor Extraordinary of Assyriology, University of Oxford, *The Religions of Ancient Egypt and Babylonia*, Edinburgh, 1902 [27, 149]

SHERRINGTON, CHARLES SCOTT (1857-1952), Edinburgh, 1937-8, Sometime Professor of Physiology, University of Oxford, *Man on his Nature*, Cambridge, 1940 [110]

213

SODERBLOM, NATHAN (1866-1931), Edinburgh, 1930-1, Archbishop of Upsala, *The Living God*, 1933 [121]

SORLEY, WILLIAM RITCHIE (1855-1935), Aberdeen, 1914-15, Knightbridge Professor of Moral Philosophy, University of Cambridge, *Moral Values and the Idea of God*, Cambridge, 1917 [72, 137, 155]

STIRLING, JAMES HUTCHISON (1820-1909), Edinburgh, 1888-90, Writer and Philosopher, *Philosophy and Theology*, Edinburgh, 1890 [2, 26, 97, 114]

STOKES, GEORGE GABRIEL (1819-1903), Edinburgh, 1891-3, Lucasian Professor of Mathematics, University of Cambridge, *Natural Theology*, two volumes, 1891 and 1893 [100, 118]

STOUT, GEORGE FREDERICK (1860-1944), Edinburgh, 1919-21, Professor of Logic and Metaphysics, University of St Andrews, *Mind and Matter*, Cambridge, 1931, *God and Nature*, Cambridge, 1952 [80, 91]

TAYLOR, ALFRED EDWARD (1869-1945), St Andrews, 1926-8, Professor of Moral Philosophy, University of Edinburgh, *The Faith of a Moralist*, two volumes, 1930 [107, 160]

TEMPLE, WILLIAM (1881-1944), Glasgow, 1932-4, Archbishop of York, *Nature, Man and God*, 1934 [6, 87, 120]

THOMSON, JOHN ARTHUR (1861-1933), St Andrews, 1915-16, Regius Professor of Natural History, University of Aberdeen, *The System of Animate Nature*, two volumes, 1920 [74]

TIELE, CORNELIUS PETRUS (1830-1902), Edinburgh, 1896-8, Professor of the History and Philosophy of Religion, University of Leyden, *Elements in the Science of Religion*, two volumes, 1897 and 1899 [101, 109]

TILLICH, PAUL (1886-1965), Aberdeen, 1953-4, Professor of Philosophical Theology, Union Theological Seminary, New York, *Systematic Theology*, volumes 2 and 3, 1957 and 1964 [92, 174]

TOYNBEE, ARNOLD JOSEPH (1889-   ), Edinburgh, 1952-3, Research Professor of International History, University of London, *An Historian's Approach to Religion*, Oxford, 1956 [51, 96]

WALLACE, WILLIAM (1844-97), Glasgow, 1893-4, Professor of Moral Philosophy, University of Oxford, *Lectures and Essays On Natural Theology and Ethics*, 1898 [5, 115]

WARD, JAMES (1843-1925), Aberdeen, 1896-8, Professor of Mental Philosophy and Logic, University of Cambridge, *Naturalism and Agnosticism*, two volumes, 1899 [14], St Andrews, 1907-10, *The Realm of Ends*, or *Pluralism and Theism*, Cambridge, 1911 [56, 75]

WATSON, JOHN (1847-1939), Glasgow, 1910-12, Professor of Moral Philosophy, Queen's University, Kingston, *The Interpretation of Religious Experience*, two volumes, Glasgow, 1912 [55]

WEBB, CLEMENT CHARLES JULIAN (1865-1954), Aberdeen, 1918-19, Fellow of Magdalen College, Oxford, *God and Personality*, 1919 [15], *Divine Personality and Human Life*, 1920 [158]

WEIZSACKER, CARL FRIEDRICH VON (1912-   ), Glasgow, 1959-61, Professor of Philosophy, University of Hamburg, *The Relevance of Science*, 1964 [113]

WHITEHEAD, ALFRED NORTH (1861-1947), Edinburgh, 1927-8, Professor of Philosophy, Harvard University, *Process and Reality*, Cambridge, 1929 [53, 82]

WRIGHT, GEORG HENRIK VON (1916-   ), Professor of Philosophy, University of Helsinki, *Norm and Action*, 1963, *The Varieties of Goodness*, 1963 [136]

Note: Baron Friedrich von Hügel accepted the invitation to give the Gifford Lectures at Edinburgh from 1924-26, but was forced to withdraw because of ill health. Some of the material he had prepared is in *The Reality of God*, 1931, which was published posthumously.

Jacques Maritain accepted the invitation to lecture at Aberdeen from 1940-1942, but war conditions prevented his delivery of the lectures. His appointment as French Ambassador to the Holy See prevented his acceptance of a renewed invitation after the war.

APPENDIX 2

Gifford Lecturers
With Titles of Lectures Not Yet Published

ARON, RAYMOND (1905-   ), Aberdeen, 1964-6, Professor, Institute d'Etudes Politiques and Sorbonne, *On Historical Consciousness in Thought and Action*, (1) *On Historical Consciousness in Thought; Understanding the Past;* (2) *On Historical Action; the Prince and the Planner*

BERGSON, HENRI (1859-1941), Edinburgh, 1913-14, Professor, College de France, *The Problem of Personality*

BOHR, NIELS HENRIK DAVID (1885-1962), Edinburgh, 1949, Director of the Institute of Theoretical Physics, Copenhagen, *Causality and Complementarity: Epistemological Lessons of Studies in Atomic Physics*

BUTTERFIELD, HERBERT (1900-   ), Glasgow, 1965-6, Regius Professor of Modern History, University of Cambridge, *Human Beliefs and the Development of Historical Writing*

CHADWICK, HENRY (1920-   ), St Andrews, 1962-4, Regius Professor of Divinity, University of Oxford, *Authority in the Early Church*

DAUBE, DAVID (1909-   ), Edinburgh, 1962-3, Regius Professor of Civil Law, University of Oxford, 1. *The Deed and the Doer in the Bible,* 2. *Law and Wisdom in the Bible*

DEMANT, VIGO AUGUSTE (1893-   ), St Andrews, 1956-8, Regius Professor of Moral and Pastoral Theology, University of Oxford, *The Penumbra of Ethics:* (1) *The Religious Climate,* (2) *The Moral Career of Christendom*

FLINT, ROBERT (1838-1907), Edinburgh, 1907, the lectures were not delivered

HENDEL, CHARLES WILLIAM (1890-   ), Glasgow, 1962-3, Formerly Professor of Philosophy, Yale University, 1. *Politics: The Trial of a Pelagian Faith,* 2. *The Limit of Human Power*

HOCKING, WILLIAM ERNEST (1873-   ), Glasgow, 1937, Professor of Philosophy, Harvard University, *Fact and Destiny*

HODGES, HERBERT ARTHUR (1905-   ), Aberdeen, 1956-7, Professor of Philosophy, University of Reading, *The Logic of Religious Thinking:* 1. *Its Customary Forms and Presuppositions.* 2. *Its Intellectual Status*

KOHLER, WOLFGANG (1887-1967), Edinburgh, 1957-8, Professor of Psychology, Swarthmore College, 1. *The Psychology of Values,* 2. *Psychology and Physics*

KRAUS, OSCAR (1872-1942), Edinburgh, 1940, Formerly Professor of Philosophy, University of Prague, *New Meditations on Mind, God and His Creation*

MACKINNON, DONALD MACKENZIE (1913-   ), Edinburgh, 1964-6, Norris-Hulse Professor of Divinity, University of Cambridge, *The Problem of Metaphysics*

McLENNAN, RODERICK DIARMID (1898-   ), Edinburgh, 1959-60, Minister, Church of Scotland, *The Unity of Moral Experience*

NOCK, ARTHUR DARBY (1902-1963), Aberdeen, 1938-40, *Hellenistic Religion—The Two Phases*

RIDGEWAY, WILLIAM (1853-1926), Aberdeen, 1909-11, Brereton Reader in Classics, University of Cambridge, *The Evolution of the Religions of Ancient Greece and Rome*

SCHWEITZER, ALBERT (1875-1965), Edinburgh, 1934, Missionary Doctor, Lambaréné, *The Problem of Natural Theology and Natural Ethics*

SMITH, JOHN ALEXANDER (1863-1939), Glasgow, 1928, Wainflete Professor of Mental Philosophy, University of Oxford, *The Heritage of Idealism*

TYLOR, EDWARD BURNETT (1832-1917), Aberdeen, 1889-91, Keeper of the University Museum and Reader in Anthropology, University of Oxford

WISDOM, JOHN (1904-   ), Aberdeen, 1948-50, Lecturer in Moral Sciences, Trinity College, Cambridge, 1. *The Mystery of the Transcendental*, 2. *The Discovery of the Transcendental*

ZAEHNER, RICHARD CHARLES (1913-   ), St Andrews, 1967-9, Spalding Professor of Eastern Religions and Ethics, All Souls College, Oxford, *Concordant Discord: The Interdependence of Faiths*

ACKNOWLEDGMENTS

Grateful acknowledgment is made to the following authors or executors, publishers and other holders of copyright for permission to use excerpts from published Gifford Lectures.

Messrs George Allen and Unwin Ltd.

Edwyn Bevan, *Symbolism and Belief* [46, 50, 90]
Brand Blanshard, *Reason and Goodness* [135]
C. A. Campbell, *On Selfhood and Godhood* [4, 49]
J. N. Findlay, *The Transcendence of the Cave* [69]
W. Heisenberg, *Physics and Philosophy* [106, 168]
Malcolm Knox, *Action* [134]
John Laird, *Mind and Deity* [18]
    Theism and Cosmology [163]
H. J. Paton, *The Modern Predicament* [3, 9, 84, 177]
H. H. Price, *Belief* [40]
C. C. J. Webb, *God and Personality* [15]
    Divine Personality and Human Life [158]

Messrs Edward Arnold (Publishers) Ltd.

W. McNeile Dixon, *The Human Situation* [111]

Bedford College, University of London

A. C. Bradley, *Ideals of Religion* [143, 161]

Messrs Ernest Benn Ltd.

C. Lloyd Morgan, *Emergent Evolution* [166]
    Life, Mind and Spirit [123]
J. A. Thomson, *The System of Animate Nature* [74]

Messrs A. and C. Black, Ltd.

A. M. Farrer, *The Freedom of the Will* [131]
James Ward, *Naturalism and Agnosticism* [14]

Messrs Basil Blackwell and Mott, Ltd.

Leonard Hodgson, *For Faith and Freedom* [95, 119]
Miss J. C. Bosanquet, *The Principle of Individuality and Value* [85]
Bernard Bosanquet, *The Value and Destiny of the Individual* [61]

Cambridge University Press

E. W. Barnes, *Scientific Theory and Religion* [65, 108, 157]
A. S. Eddington, *The Nature of the Physical World* [102, 103]
E. W. Hobson, *The Domain of Natural Science* [76, 122]
C. E. Raven, *Natural Religion and Christian Theology* [151, 164]
C. S. Sherrington, *Man on his Nature* [110]
W. R. Sorley, *Moral Values and the Idea of God* [72, 137, 155]

G. F. Stout, *God and Nature* [80, 91]
A. N. Whitehead, *Process and Reality* [53, 82]

Miss Clare Campbell

James Ward, *The Realm of Ends* [56, 75]

The Clarendon Press

L. R. Farnell, *Greek Hero Cults* [145]
                The Attributes of God [48, 70]
H. H. Henson, *Christian Morality, Natural, Developing, Final* [33, 141]
Werner Jaeger, *The Theology of the Early Greek Philosophers* [8]
R. R. Marett, *Faith, Hope and Charity in Primitive Religion* [24]
                Sacraments of Simple Folk [147]
A. S. Pringle-Pattison, *The Idea of God in the Light of Recent Philosophy* [47]
                The Idea of Immortality [156]
                Studies in the Philosophy of Religion [129]
W. D. Ross, *Foundations of Ethics* [132, 133]

Messrs T. and T. Clark

A. H. Sayce, *The Religions of Ancient Egypt and Babylonia* [27, 149]

Messrs Collins, Sons and Co., Ltd.

Alister Hardy, *The Living Stream* [112]
             The Divine Flame [20, 175]
C. F. von Weizsacker, *The Relevance of Science* [113]

Messrs Gerald Duckworth and Co. Ltd.

E. Boutroux, *Science and Religion in Contemporary Philosophy* [104]

Edinburgh University Press

Rudolf Bultmann, *History and Eschatology* [93, 176]

Messrs Faber and Faber Ltd.

John Macmurray, *The Self as Agent* [127, 170]
                Persons in Relation [171]

Harvard University Press

R. B. Perry, *Realms of Value* [60, 139, 173]

The Harvill Press Ltd.

Gabriel Marcel, *The Mystery of Being* [78, 94, 152]

Messrs Hodder and Stoughton, Ltd.

Karl Barth, *The Knowledge of God and the Service of God* [10, 45]
J. S. Haldane, *The Sciences and Philosophy* [126, 167]
W. P. Paterson, *The Nature of Religion* [89]

Messrs Hodder and Stoughton and the Estate of A. J. Balfour

A. J. Balfour, *Theism and Humanism* [17]
Theism and Thought [13]

Messrs MacDonald and Evans Ltd.

W. G. de Burgh, *From Morality to Religion* [64, 144]

Messrs MacMillan and Co. Ltd.

S. Alexander, *Space Time and Deity* [165]
W. W. Fowler, *The Religious Experience of the Roman People* [29]
Henry Jones, *A Faith that Enquires* [57, 73]
William Mitchell, *The Place of Minds in the World* [162]
Alexander Macbeath, *Experiments in Living* [140]
A. E. Taylor, *The Faith of a Moralist* [107, 160]

Messrs MacMillan and Co. Ltd. and Mrs Temple

William Temple, *Nature, Man and God* [6, 87, 120]

Messrs MacMillan and Co. (New York)

Richard Kroher, *The Primacy of Faith* [62, 63]
R. A. Lanciani, *New Tales of Old Rome* [32]
A. N. Whitehead, *Process and Reality* [53, 82]

Messrs Longmans, Green and Co. Ltd.

W. R. Inge, *The Philosophy of Plotinus* [68, 154]

Messrs John Murray

Charles Gore, *The Philosophy of the Good Life* [77]
W. M. Ramsay, *Asianic Elements in Greek Civilization* [83]
R. B. Haldane, *The Pathway to Reality* [41, 52]

Messrs James Nisbet and Co. Ltd.

Emil Brunner, *Christianity and Civilization* [67, 142, 172]
H. H. Farmer, *Revelation and Religion* [19, 153]
Paul Tillich, *Systematic Theology* [92, 174]
Reinhold Niebuhr, *The Nature and Destiny of Man* [36, 71]

Oxford University Press

John Baillie, *The Sense of the Presence of God* [39, 44, 116]
Nathan Soderblom, *The Living God* [121]
Arnold Toynbee, *An Historian's Approach to Religion* [51, 96]

Messrs G. P. Putnam's Sons

John Dewey, *The Quest for Certainty* [130, 138]

Messrs Routledge and Kegan Paul Ltd.

M. Polanyi, *Personal Knowledge* [124, 169]
G. H. von Wright, *The Varieties of Goodness* [136]

Messrs Sheed and Ward

Etienne Gilson, *The Spirit of Mediaeval Philosophy* [12, 35, 99]

The Society of Authors

Christopher Dawson, *Religion and Culture* [38]
Religion and the Rise of Western Culture [34]

Trinity College Cambridge

J. G. Frazer, *Belief in Immortality* [148]
The Worship of Nature [22, 23]

The University of Aberdeen

Hans Driesch, *Science and Philosophy of Organism* [105]

Grateful acknowledgment is also made to the following American publishers, where separate rights for America and Canada are involved.

Messrs Harper and Row

Werner Heisenberg, *Physics and Philosophy* [106, 108]
John Macmurray, *Persons in Relation* [171]

Humanities Press Inc.

Malcolm Knox, *Action* [134]
H. H. Price, *Belief* [40]
G. H. von Wright, *The Varieties of Goodness* [136]

Messrs Charles Scribner's Sons

Emil Brunner, *Christianity and Civilization* [67, 142, 172]
Reinhold Niebuhr, *The Nature and Destiny of Man* [36, 71]

The Shoe String Press

John Laird, *Mind and Deity* [18]

University of Chicago Press

Michael Polanyi, *Personal Knowledge* [124, 169]
Paul Tillich, *Systematic Theology* [92, 174]

INDEX

(References to extracts from the particular author are printed in *italics*.)